D1111988

STOP
THE
TRAFFIK

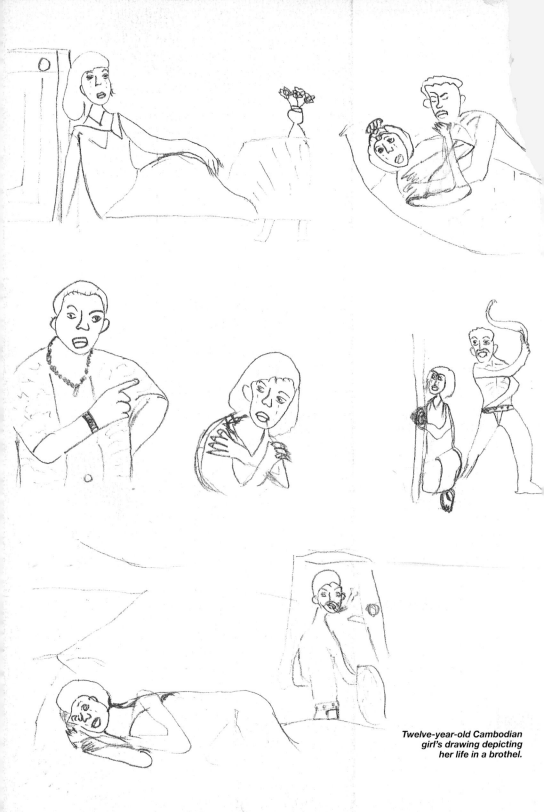

Twelve-year-old Cambodian girl's drawing depicting her life in a brothel.

STOP
THE
TRAFFIK

PEOPLE SHOULDN'T
BE BOUGHT & SOLD

STEVE CHALKE

with a chapter by

CHERIE BLAIR

Copyright © 2009 Steve Chalke
Chapter 2 copyright © Cherie Blair
This edition copyright © 2009 Lion Hudson

The authors assert the moral right
to be identified as the authors of this work

A Lion Book
imprint of
Lion Hudson plc
Wilkinson House, Jordan Hill Road,
Oxford, OX2 8DR, England
www.lionhudson.com

ISBN 978-0-7459-5358-8 (UK)
ISBN 978-0-8254-7846-8 (US)

DISTRIBUTED BY
UK: Marston Book Service, PO Box 269,
Abingdon, Oxon, OX14 4YN
USA: Trafalgar Square Publishing,
814 N. Franklin Street, Chicago, IL 60610
USA Christian Market: Kregel Publications,
PO Box 2607, Grand Rapids,
Michigan 49501

First edition 2009
10 9 8 7 6 5 4 3 2 1 0

A catalogue record for this book is available
from the British Library

Typeset in 9/11 Helvetica Neue
Printed and bound in China

IMPORTANT NOTE: *All the commissioned photography in this book has been taken in the studio and posed by models. The models should not be identified as the characters in real-life case studies unless otherwise stated.*

CONTENTS

FOREWORD ◢

'Two years ago everything changed. I was trafficked. I was fooled. I was deceived by a man who said that he loved me. The tragedy is that I believed him.

Now I know that love is not shown by forcing me to work on the streets, beating me up, force feeding me and turning me into someone with no mind of my own. I had become like a frightened rabbit. I was terrified that he would kill me. Death too often felt like my only way to escape.

But I am a survivor.

I can't believe that I am sitting writing a foreword to a book to empower others.

Trafficking isn't a distant crime. It's right here. There is no escape from the fact that people are being bought and sold, across all borders, continents, around your town and even up your street.

People are product.

I was one of them.

Now I am part of the STOP THE TRAFFIK campaign. This book is for anyone who wants more than just facts about the shame of this trade in people. It's for those who want to do something to end it.

I have a new life but I am haunted by the faces of those who used me, those whom I did not choose, those for whom I was nothing more than a ten-minute thing.

Please join STOP THE TRAFFIK and make a difference to people's lives...

... people like me.'

A survivor of trafficking

CHAPTER 1

STOP

Article 4 of the universal declaration of human rights says that people should not be bought and sold. And yet today the trafficking of people is the fastest-growing global crime.

'I am Sunni. I am seven years old. I've just been sold for ten pounds.'

WIHINI, AGED NINE, AND HER BROTHER SUNNI, AGED SEVEN, lived on Thane train station in Mumbai, India with their parents – both alcoholics. Wihini and Sunni went to a day centre, where they learnt to read and write and were given the chance to play.

One day Wihini and Sunni simply didn't turn up. Street children often tend to disappear for days, as they try to scrape a living sweeping long-distance trains, but they had been attending the centre daily for three months, so when a week or so went by the project staff became worried, and went in search of their parents.

The workers found the father lying drunk on the station platform. When they roused him and asked about the children, he admitted that a man had come to him one morning offering money for them. He needed money for alcohol, so he agreed. The trafficker had taken Wihini and Sunni away for the equivalent of just £20.

The father was angry because he had never received his money. Their mother wouldn't speak about it. The children were never seen again.

What happened to Wihini and Sunni? Nobody knows. In that area of Mumbai, children often disappeared. They are kidnapped or sold into prostitution, forced labour, adoption or even child sacrifice. The workers at the Asha Deep centre had seen this before.

But this was once too often. Phil Lane, my friend who worked in a slum community, first told me this story a few years ago. He was so deeply affected by what had happened to Wihini and Sunni that he knew he had to do all he could to prevent it happening to others.

'The story was picked up and passed on and as evidence gathered we realized this is happening on a huge scale, around the world – even on our own doorstep. Not 200 years ago. Not even fifty years ago. It was – and is – happening today.'

STEVE CHALKE, *FOUNDER*

And so STOP THE TRAFFIK was born.

HUMAN TRAFFICKING
A definition

Human trafficking is the dislocation of someone by deception or coercion for exploitation, through forced prostitution, forced labour, or other forms of slavery.

A more thorough, and widely accepted, definition was put together by the United Nations Office on Drugs and Crime (UNODC) in what is commonly called the Palermo Protocol, of 2000:

For the purposes of this Protocol:

(a) 'Trafficking in persons' shall mean the recruitment, transportation, transfer, harbouring or receipt of persons, by means of the threat or use of force or other forms of coercion, of abduction, of fraud, of deception, of the abuse of power or of a position of vulnerability or of the giving or receiving of payments or benefits to achieve the consent of a person having control over another person, for the purpose of exploitation. Exploitation shall include, at a minimum, the exploitation of the prostitution of others or other forms of sexual exploitation, forced labour or services, slavery or practices similar to slavery, servitude or the removal of organs;

(b) The consent of a victim of trafficking in persons to the intended exploitation set forth in subparagraph (a) of this article shall be irrelevant where any of the means set forth in subparagraph (a) have been used;

(c) The recruitment, transportation, transfer, harbouring or receipt of a child for the purpose of exploitation shall be considered 'trafficking in persons' even if this does not involve any of the means set forth in subparagraph (a) of this article;

(d) 'Child' shall mean any person under eighteen years of age.

In the time it has taken you to read this chapter so far, as many as twelve children have been trafficked – for sex.

Thane Railway Station, Mumbai, India.

Street children sleeping on a pavement near Thane Railway station, Mumbai, India.

800,000 people are trafficked across borders each year

US STATE DEPARTMENT

It is estimated that two children per minute are trafficked for sexual exploitation.

UNICEF believes that this amounts to an estimated 1.2 million children trafficked every year.

In 2004, between 14,500 and 17,500 people were trafficked into the United States

US STATE DEPARTMENT

Human trafficking generates between 10 and 12 billion dollars a year.

UNICEF

Total profit from human trafficking is second only to the trafficking of drugs.

THE EUROPEAN POLICE OFFICE; EURPOL

The numbers tell you the huge scale of this problem. But behind each number is a sea of faces. Behind the statistics are mothers and fathers, husbands and wives, sons and daughters, brothers and sisters, torn apart by trafficking; these are innocent lives ruined by abuse.

These are human rights violations on a grotesque scale. And the problem is getting worse.

Villages in rural China have been decimated by trafficking. This man's wife was trafficked, leaving him to care for his young daughter, whom he fears will be vulnerable to trafficking when she is older. Read his story on page 136.

VERA'S STORY

At the age of twenty-seven, an Albanian girl, Vera, was mugged and raped in her house in Albania and then kidnapped. She was then locked up in a house in Albania for two days and transported by bus to Greece, from where she was taken to Italy by boat. In Italy she was first pushed into a truck and then transported by train via France to Belgium. Upon arrival in Belgium she was forced into prostitution in the red light district of Antwerp. She believed she was sending all her earnings to her father in Albania. But her father never received any money. Somebody else intercepted the money in Albania and kept it.

There are many like Vera. They are beaten, raped, kidnapped, taken on journey after journey, forced into prostitution, suffering abuse after abuse.

And many are sold not once, but countless times, passed from man to man like a shared cigarette. Used, and then, all too often, stubbed out.

PAYOKE

THERE IS A DIFFERENCE
Prostitution versus forced prostitution

There is a difference between prostitution as a chosen way to earn money, and the trafficking of women into the sex trade.

Prostitution is an area of heated debate as to whether women are being drawn into a form of work that is beneath their dignity, or whether they have every right to choose to earn their money in this way if they wish.

STOP THE TRAFFIK's priority is to protect those women who are forced into sex by traffickers.

It is not only women who are affected by trafficking. Young, under-age girls are often violated in exactly the same, brutal way that Vera was. Sometimes even their virginity is sold to the highest bidder.

From a tender age, these girls grow up thinking they are worthless. They believe all they are here for is to be used as sex objects – and nothing more. Their childhood is ruined by physical, emotional and psychological violence. Far from home, used again and again, never paid; they can hardly remember anything else.

ANNA'S STORY

Anna was sold when she was twelve – by her parents.

She came from Bulgaria, but ended up in the Dutch town of Groningen, forced to work as a prostitute.

Anna is now sixteen, and her case is not unique. Many other Bulgarian girls and women are trafficked into the Netherlands, forced to work as prostitutes, in brothels and sitting in windows. They cannot keep the money they earn.

In Anna's case, the traffickers may have been tracked down by the police. Two men were arrested, and a 41-year-old Bulgarian was handed over to the Netherlands authorities. The second suspect was a 61-year-old from Groningen who was suspected of having transported and guarded these girls and women: the police expect more arrests.

But this success is only an isolated case. More has to be done to stop vulnerable under-age girls such as Anna being sold and abused.

SOURCE: DUTCH NEWSPAPER,
DAGBLAD VAN HET NOORDEN, BY MICK VAN WELY

'If to be feelingly alive to the sufferings of my fellow-creatures is to be a fanatic, I am one of the most incurable fanatics ever permitted to be at large.'

WILLIAM WILBERFORCE

In 2007 the world commemorated 200 years since the abolition of the trans-Atlantic slave trade. We heard of the horrors endured by slaves crammed into British ships, struggling through voyages to American plantations and mines where yet more suffering awaited them.

Figures such as British politician William Wilberforce and former slave Olaudah Equianou, who helped convey the abolitionist message with such power, were celebrated for refusing to accept injustice. The assumption was that we would now live in a more civilized age, with the shameful story of slavery far behind us, that nothing like it could happen today.

But slavery, especially trafficking, has not been consigned to the history books. On the contrary it is alive and thriving, on a scale that is bigger and more brutal than ever before, throughout the world. Today.

The slave trade is prohibited under Article 4 of the Universal Declaration of Human Rights. Yet the modern-day slave trade that is human trafficking is the fastest-growing form of organized crime.

TULSI'S STORY

Born in the city of Chennai, India, Tulsi was ten years old when her parents were both killed in a tragic accident. Tulsi was then taken in by an aunt. Her aunt was poor, couldn't support her, and eventually married her off at the age of sixteen. Over the next few years, Tulsi gave birth to two children; both boys, who are now three and five years old.

Tulsi's husband found it difficult to find employment and eventually took to alcohol. Already living in poverty but now facing mounting debts aggravated by his drinking habit, he borrowed heavily. Then, one night, he simply disappeared; she has never seen him since. Later that week, when the local, Mafioso-style, debt collectors called, Tulsi was to discover the extent of her husband's betrayal. Before abandoning her, he had taken out another very large loan against their home, for which he named her as a co-guarantor. Now, the obligation was all hers. In order to try to begin to pay off her debt and feed her growing boys, Tulsi was forced to turn to working as a rag-picker just to survive.

Then tragedy struck again. Her youngest son, still a baby, became ill and was diagnosed with a hole in the heart; because medical care is very expensive, Tulsi now found herself in an impossible situation. The money she was earning was nowhere near enough to make the repayments on her existing commitments over which she was already being threatened regularly. There was no way in which she could possibly afford the treatment that her son so desperately needed.

SACMEP rescued girls from the sex room of this brothel in India.

Suddenly, out of the blue, just when Tulsi felt that she couldn't carry on and that she didn't have a friend in the world, what seemed like the life-saving financial help she needed arrived from an unexpected source. A man from her village came to visit her. He explained that he knew of her dilemma and wanted to help. He told her that he could find her a job in the city of Hyderabad working as a waitress in a restaurant, and that if she would take the job he could loan her some of the money for her son's life-saving medical care up front as well as for the repayments on her home. Her part would be to agree to send back a set percentage of her earnings, month by month, in order to cover this new loan, which would be charged with a high rate of interest. Torn between abandoning her children and watching her youngest son waste away and die, she had no choice but to accept the job.

She left both her sons in the care of her neighbours, hurriedly said goodbye to her friends and climbed on board the truck that was headed for Hyderabad the following day, with other women from the city who had also been offered the opportunity of finding work away from home.

But Tulsi was never to reach Hyderabad. Instead, the truck she was transported on arrived, some days later, on the other side of India in the city of Mumbai. Here, she discovered that her employment would not be in the catering industry but in the sex trade. Imprisoned in a crowded brothel, pushed around, treated like a thing rather than a person, she was forced to offer sexual services to men night after night. Month by month, she sent some of the money she earned home in order to pay off the loan for her son's treatment and her house as well as her two boys' ongoing care – the vast majority was kept by the brothel's owner.

For two years Tulsi worked in that brothel, faithfully sending as much money as she could possibly afford home each month but never revealing to her neighbours where she actually was or how she was being forced to live.

In January 2006, the Mumbai city police raided the brothel where Tulsi was imprisoned and took her, and the ten other girls who worked there, into custody.

I [Steve Chalke] met her a few days later, along with doctors working with Oasis India. Oasis is regularly allowed into the centre where Tulsi was being held, to provide health care and support. As we talked together, and slowly her story emerged, Tulsi, now twenty-three, wept with the tears that only a mother separated from her children can ever fully understand. Oasis India has agreed to go to court for her and to offer to house her in their safe-house in Mumbai. At the same time, they will try to make contact with her community back in Chennai, where they also work, to discover more about her son's condition, arrange for her supported and safe return home and offer her training and ongoing employment when she arrives.

Tulsi's story continues…

Business begins about 4 p.m. in the Mumbai brothels, such as this one on Falkland Road.

The trading of slaves was outlawed 200 years ago, yet it still thrives today – and we want to eradicate it altogether.

The vulnerable, such as Anna and Tulsi, should be free to live their lives safe from the risk of being captured and sold. Living with that freedom should not be a luxury enjoyed by only a privileged few. It is a fundamental human right, owed to every person around the world.

> **'When the rulers are silent before injustice, then the evil hand of violence is not far off. The violent language of human hands is fearful when there is no justice.'**
>
> **DIETRICH BONHOEFFER,** *MEDITATIONS ON PSALMS*

It is not enough that trafficking is illegal. Laws reflect an official stance, but do little to prevent determined crime, especially when so much money is at stake. Trafficking is on the increase. And that means that governments, industries, and the UN itself – what Bonhoeffer calls 'the rulers' – need to do more to stop the traffickers, who deal daily in 'the violent language of human hands'.

TAKING ACTION
Declarations

In February 2008, more than 1.5 million declarations from every continent in the world were delivered to the United Nations, calling for more to be done to:

▲ **Prevent the sale of people**
▲ **Protect those affected by trafficking**
▲ **Prosecute the traffickers.**

A new relationship developed. Now STOP THE TRAFFIK works with the United Nations Office on Drugs and Crime (UNODC) to produce resources for, and connections to, grassroots communities around the world.

The challenge to stop the trafficking now has support and membership throughout the world.

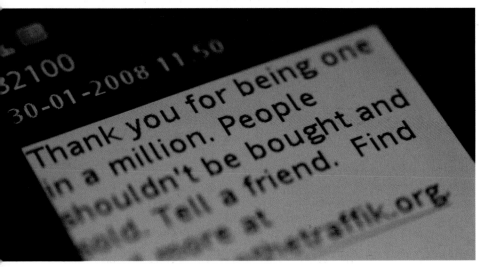

The number '1.5 million' shows you the huge response to this problem. People across the globe are motivated to act to stop the trafficking of people.

Each of those 1.5 million people who supported the STOP THE TRAFFIK Global Declaration is an individual. All they did was sign a petition. Yet that small, step, when taken by enough people, has enabled the start of an exciting new relationship between STOP THE TRAFFIK and the UN which, together, are determined to end trafficking.

Just as the small step of signing a petition made so much difference, there are many small steps – as well as bigger actions – you can make in your everyday life that will help bring the tyranny of trafficking to an end.

This book will show you how you can make a difference.

Still wondering if you, one person, can make a difference to this global crime?

To illustrate just how big a difference one, individual voice saying 'Stop' can make, here is a vivid story told by Steve Chalke on 13 February 2008, from the platform at the opening session of the UN.GIFT conference in Vienna – in the presence of all the nations of the world:

THE LITTLE MONK

Gladiatorial games were popular in ancient Rome. The gladiators, the vast majority of whom were slaves, many of them what we would now refer to as trafficked people, were often forced to fight to the death as entertainment for the bloodthirsty crowds that packed into the huge stadium known as the Coliseum. But in early January AD 403 that was about to change.

As far back as AD 327, Emperor Constantine had tried to outlaw the gladiatorial fights across his far-flung empire. More than one of his successors had attempted to do the same. But, with the empire's capital now transferred to Constantinople, the citizens of Rome, who despised the new ways of the changing empire, were defiant and determined to keep them.

Telemachus, a young monk from what we now know as modern-day Turkey, along with ever-growing numbers across the empire, was deeply disturbed by the barbarity of the 'games'. He could not understand how the Emperor Honorius, who sponsored the contests, claimed to be a Christian, as did tens of thousands of those who regularly took seats in the audience. However, he realized that talking about this evil was not enough – for him, it was time to stand up and cry 'Stop!'.

The 'little monk', as former American President Ronald Reagan referred to him in a famous White House speech, decided to travel to Rome to make his protest. On his arrival he found the city in festive mood with a gladiatorial circus in full swing. The next day he followed the vast throng of spectators – some 80,000 people, into the Coliseum, but faced with the horror of watching the carnage in the arena whilst a fever pitch crowd bayed for more blood, he couldn't just sit there and watch. Rising from his seat, at the top of his voice he shouted: 'Stop, stop, in the name of Christ, stop.' And then, constantly repeating his cry, he began to make his way down, through the crowds, to the floor of the stadium.

At first the crowd responded to the scrawny figure of the 21-year-old monk running frantically about the arena – ducking and weaving between the combatants – as a kind of comedy extra. They were used to theatrical novelties being laid on by the organizers of the games and so they initially laughed and applauded his antics. However, as they began to digest the impact of his words and his real intent, their mood quickly changed – now they hissed, booed and bellowed at him at the top of their voices. Eventually they began to hurl stones and other rubbish at him to the point where two of the gladiators, keen for their own sakes to keep the crowd on their side, joined them by lunging at him with their swords and batons.

When the frenzy was over, the 'little monk' lay dead in the middle of the arena. The huge crowd fell silent. Then, after a minute or so, as the horror of what they had just been part of began to sink in, first as a trickle, then a stream and finally as an unstoppable torrent, they rose from their seats and, without speaking, began to leave the stadium. It was as though the young monk's last cry was still echoing around the giant arena.

Amazing Change partnered STOP THE TRAFFIK in gathering the 1.5 milllion signatures.

Just days later, the Emperor Honorius issued an edict that finally ended all future gladiatorial games. And, although the scholars still argue over whether he would have bowed to the voice of this single abolitionist, without doubt the 'little monk' became the catalyst for long-needed change. Telemachus' bravery in taking on the system and finding the courage to shout 'Stop' at the top of his voice, galvanized the silent majority into action and, as a result, never again would any gladiator die in the Coliseum or elsewhere in the empire.

At the beginning of the twenty-first century, human trafficking now ranks as one of the biggest challenges to human rights that our world faces and is the fastest growing source of organized crime.

In 2006 a determined group of volunteers asked ordinary people across the UK and the rest of the world to shout 'Stop'. The response to that challenge means that STOP THE TRAFFIK is now a global movement numbering more than 1,000 member organizations, including churches, schools, colleges, businesses, local charities, national non-govenmental organizations (NGOs), community groups and other faith groups, with a presence in a quarter of the world's countries.

TAKING ACTION
Goals

Our daring goal was to work to raise 1 million signatures calling on individual governments and the United Nations to work together towards common goals, to:

- ◢ **Prevent the sale of people**
- ◢ **Protect the victims**
- ◢ **Prosecute the traffickers.**

We gathered more than 1.5 million signatures from around the world. The sheer size of this grassroots petition, drawn from the old and the young, men and women, of every continent on Earth, speaks for itself. Human trafficking is a crime that shames us all.

1.5 MILLION
PEOPLE AROUND THE WORLD WANT TO END PEOPLE TRAFFICKING

Delivery of the declaration to the UN.

The story of Telemachus shows us the power of a single voice. What is even better for us today is that we can make choices that involve a fraction of the sacrifice made by the 'little monk'. Telemachus died crying 'Stop'. But we all have the power to cry 'Stop' in ways that are simple, practical and effective.

And one of those steps is simply reading this book to inform ourselves. Our awareness of trafficking will broaden and the next stop, the next choice will become clear. These everyday choices will represent our own, powerful cry of 'STOP', which means that those people affected by trafficking have hope; the hope of living as we are meant to live, with our human rights intact.

> **We can make a difference.**
> **Together, we can STOP THE TRAFFIK.**

STOP THE TRAFFIK was formed to raise awareness, encourage involvement and inspire action to help stop human trafficking, and to support those it affects.

For more ideas visit:

www.stopthetraffik.org

WOMEN

'I come to the monstrous scandal of human trafficking through my work as a British lawyer... I am determined to do all I can to remove the barriers blocking the progress of women.'

HUMAN RIGHTS

There is, of course, no more basic human right than freedom from slavery. In fact, it was the very first human right recognized by international law. Britain outlawed the Atlantic slave trade just over two hundred years ago. This was followed by an outright ban on slavery throughout the British Empire. Subsequently, in the last two centuries, there have been something like eighty international conventions and documents aimed at stopping the vile practice of slavery and its modern form of trafficking. This clearly demonstrates the world's revulsion at this inhumanity.

International law makes clear that those responsible for enslavement are guilty of a crime against humanity and are viewed as enemies of all people. Their actions put them beyond the protection of any individual country and make them liable – like the torturer – to arrest and prosecution by the International Criminal Court. But it is also a mark of just how profitable this evil trade is and the difficulty of enforcing the law that the trafficking and ownership of human beings continues on a huge and shameful scale.

I have no doubt that William Wilberforce and his fellow campaigners would be both shocked and appalled if they knew the staggering statistics of slavery so many years after his death.

The International Labour Organization (ILO) estimates that US $10 billion is derived from the initial 'sale' of individuals, with the remainder representing the estimated profits from the activities or goods produced by the victims of this barbaric crime.

A girl is forced into a car by traffickers.

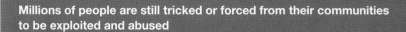

HUMAN TRAFFICKING
The statistics

Millions of people are still tricked or forced from their communities to be exploited and abused

At any one time, it is estimated that over 2.5 million are recruited, entrapped, transported and exploited within enforced labour as a result of trafficking within countries, or between them

The trafficking trade in all in its many forms nets an estimated $32 billion dollars each year for the traffickers

US $10 billion is derived from the initial 'sale' of individuals, with the remainder representing the estimated profits from the activities or goods produced by the victims of this barbaric crime.

Human trafficking knows no boundaries. Almost every country in the world is affected, either as a source, transit or destination for victims. But there is a danger that this very scale numbs our response or drives us into despair. That is why the individual stories, which are such a feature of this book, are so important and demand our anger and our action. It is these accounts of hopes crushed and lives ruined which must shake us out of our lethargy and despair.

FEMALE TRAFFICKING

Time and time again – as this book shows – it is the female voices we hear. This should be no surprise. Women and girls, of course, make up the overwhelming majority of victims trafficked for sex. Their destinations include cities and towns up and down the UK and around the world. A recent investigation by the British newspaper *The Guardian* showed the heartbreaking fate of hundreds of Chinese girls, some as young as eleven, brought to the UK, where their dreams of a better life ended in brothels in our communities. Similar stories could be told about too many communities in too many countries.

Girl in Bangkok selling flowers. Most of the flower girls come from Cambodia and Vietnam with a family member to sell items in bars. Some of these girls will be trafficked. They work in the red light areas until midnight or 1 a.m. and are very vulnerable.

ECONOMIC EXPLOITATION ◢

According to the ILO, women and girls are also the majority of those economically exploited in other ways, in sweatshops or as domestic servants. Trafficking, like poverty, discrimination and abuse of human rights, wears a woman's face. Indeed, the two are strongly related. It is the prejudice that women face in many parts of the world, their lack of rights and control over their own lives, which helps create the conditions where trafficking can flourish. Women – and children – are the key target group of the traffickers exactly because of their marginalization, their poverty and their exclusion from employment and educational opportunities. This is why we must see the urgent need to step up efforts to combat trafficking as part of the wider battle for human rights, and those of women in particular.

This is timely. For, along with the recent celebration of the 200th anniversary of the ending of the trans-Atlantic slave trade, we have recently marked another very significant anniversary. Sixty years ago, the international community agreed the Universal Declaration of Human Rights. This was a remarkable response to the horrors of the Holocaust and the Second World War and signalled a determination to build a better world.

Led by the inimitable Eleanor Roosevelt, wife of the former US President Franklin D. Roosevelt, and drawn up by experts from across the world, the Declaration clearly set out the basic rights that belong to us all, whatever our background and whatever our country, simply because of our common humanity. In December 1948, it was adopted by the founding members of the United Nations. Proudly proclaiming in Article 4: 'no one shall be held in slavery or servitude; slavery and the slave shall be prohibited in all their forms', it was a huge step forward for the world.

Esther Benjamins Trust (EBT) is committed to ending the trafficking of Nepalese children into abusive and exploitative Indian circuses. EBT Retrieval teams regularly visit circuses to rescue trafficked children. After reuniting the children with their families, they provide long-term support.

But just as Wilberforce would be shocked to see the size of the modern-day slave trade, so the authors of the Declaration would, I believe, be appalled that their ambitions are so far from realization. Across the world, there are still tens of millions living in fear and hunger, denied even the most basic human rights. While both men and women suffer from this denial of the dignity of life, the facts show that women are particularly badly affected:

WOMEN'S RIGHTS
The facts

70% of the world's poor are female, according to the United Nations

Two out of three illiterate adults are women (UNESCO Institute for Statistics, 2005)

Less than 2% of titled land in the developing world is owned by women (International Finance Corporation... Gender Equal Land Laws)

Half a million women a year die as a result of pregnancy or childbirth (UNICEF, 2008).

Thus the discrimination which women suffer can be seen in many forms, from the cradle to the grave. You see it, for example, in the cultures that encourage families to value boys, which can lead to abortions or even infanticide of baby girls. You can see it in those societies which limit educational opportunities for girls, forcing them to remain trapped inside the home instead of preparing them for a life in the outside world. You see it, too, in child brides, in forced marriages and in the many societies that turn a blind eye to domestic violence. It also exists in the plight in India and other countries of widows who are pushed to the very fringes of society, denied the right to inherit their husband's assets.

Gender gaps vary from place to place, but the overall pattern of women's disadvantage remains clear – and women around the world know it. A woman in a Nairobi slum summed it up when asked by a development worker what event she would change in her life if she could. She replied: 'I would be born a man.'

It is in these conditions that traffickers select their victims and peddle their lies. By reinforcing a culture where women and girls are seen as commodities or possessions and lacking the worth of their male counterparts, they help create the conditions where this trade can flourish.

By taking steps to root out these prejudices and practices, we can help combat trafficking, increase real choices for women and, importantly, improve the wealth and health of their societies.

THE EDUCATION OF WOMEN

One of these steps is the improvement in access to education to increase women's opportunities and to limit their vulnerability to the false promises of the traffickers. The benefits of educating girls go, of course, far further than this. It is simply the best investment, as repeated studies have shown, that any country can make, for it is directly linked to higher economic productivity, better health, lower infant mortality, higher returns on investment, even higher agricultural yields.

Education is not the answer to everything, as it must be linked to job opportunities and equality in all areas. But it is one of the key elements in a strategy to reduce human trafficking. Enabling girls to be educated to at least secondary level does more than open up new opportunities and choices for them. It also creates a more prosperous country, combating the poverty that makes the promises of the traffickers so difficult to resist. It will also give them a stronger voice within their communities, giving them more power over decisions at local and national level.

However, we have a long way to go. There are still five men, for example, for every woman elected to the world's parliaments. But the greater the say women have over decision-making, the more progress there will be in bringing in policies and changing attitudes that contribute to the vulnerability of women being trafficked.

This is something specifically recognized by UN.GIFT, as well as the new Women Leaders' Council, whose aim is to help push forward the agenda on women's rights and to provide a resource for advice and mentoring for women around the world to help combat trafficking. If women have more political clout, it will help, for example, step up efforts to tackle violence and abuse in the home.

VIOLENCE AGAINST WOMEN

It is a sad fact, but research has found that the majority of girls and women who have been trafficked into Europe were abused as children, either by their family or in their local community (Cathy Zimmermann and others, *Stolen Smiles; A summary report on the Physical and Psychological Health Consequences of Women and Adolescents Trafficked in Europe*, London School of Medicine and Tropical Medicine, 2006). Their lack of self-worth and desperation to escape their situations makes them easy prey for the traffickers and their local spotters. We therefore need to create a culture where people no longer stay silent about the abuse they are suffering and where the legal systems take such violence seriously. If violence and sexual abuse in the home or community is tolerated, it is easier for men to see women as commodities and accept them being bought and sold.

It may seem that changing the culture on domestic violence is an impossible challenge, but we must remember how attitudes in the UK have been transformed inside three decades. When I started practising as a young barrister some thirty years ago, it was clear that neither the police nor courts took domestic violence as seriously as they took attacks on strangers. It was a reflection of views in society as a whole that what went on behind closed doors within families was not the business of anyone else. Now the authorities and society see such domestic violence as the cowardly, despicable crime it is.

If we can see such a transformation in attitudes in the UK and in many other countries in such a short time, we can see it elsewhere. Even in the Democratic Republic of Congo (DRC), which has perhaps the worst record of sexual violence in the world, the culture is slowly being changed. Courageous women helped by grassroots groups and with outside legal advice, are now standing up to help bring their attackers to justice. UN officials say the number of rapes, though still appallingly high, had begun to come down before the latest outbreak of fighting and appalling brutality. And by giving women more protection over their own bodies, it will also help reduce the spread of HIV/AIDS that is having such devastating impact on many countries in the developing world.

It is, of course, far harder to root out violence in the home or community if violence is all around, as is the case in the DRC. Many of the countries that provide the main source of victims are scarred by conflict, ethnic tensions and civil war. It is these conflicts and the increased poverty and despair they bring which lead to many seeking a better life elsewhere, whatever the risks.

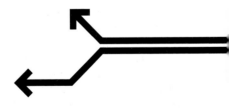

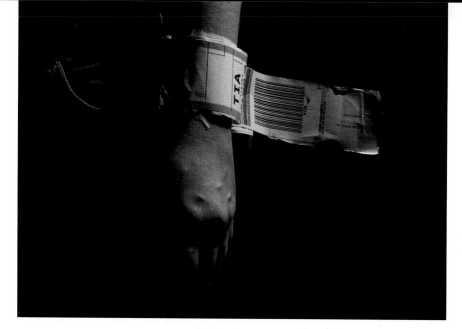

Conflict leaves a legacy of lawlessness, destruction and economic instability as well as rising numbers of orphans and widows. It also leads to violence being seen as the norm, where rape and abuse are commonplace and where the breakdown of society means the attackers are unlikely to face any sanction. Such sexual violence has, as we have seen across the world, become institutionalized, with girls and women taken captive to serve as sex slaves – as well, of course, as being coerced into fighting. Trafficking within borders is just as evil and just as damaging as that which crosses continents or national borders.

We need to step up efforts to tackle the source of conflicts that lead to such increases in violence, as well as increased mass migration and economic misery.

WHAT WE CAN DO

The reality is, of course, that we are not going to stop migration. It is important for the prosperity of many destination countries, just as many of the source countries depend on the money sent back from abroad. We must work within our own countries to improve protections for migrants and particularly for women who are far more likely to work on the margins of society.

As Radhika Coomaraswamy, former UN Special Rapporteur on Violence Against Women, has pointed out, traffickers fish in the stream of migration, 'preying on the most vulnerable to supply to the most exploitative, hazardous and inhuman forms of work'. This must involve more than increased action against the criminals behind this trade and exploitation. We must also offer more support to the victims, including protection schemes, safe houses and assistance schemes. It is important, too, to remember that they are not criminals but victims of an appalling crime. They deserve and need our sympathy and help, not our condemnation.

When women return to their own countries, we must ensure they can return in safety with dignity and support to reduce the risk of them falling prey again to the traffickers, as has happened too many times in the past. Many countries in recent years have taken major steps to putting in place sensitive assistance schemes, but there is more to be done.

There is also a great deal more to do both at national and international level to crack down on trafficking, to free those held in modern-day slavery and to bring those responsible to justice.

We now, in general, have the international agreements and domestic laws in place. Well over 100 countries, including the UK, have now signed and ratified the UN Trafficking Protocol, which calls for cooperation and action to prevent, suppress and punish human trafficking. The International Criminal Court has also made clear that it regards enslavement as one of the serious offences, which will warrant investigation and prosecution.

This woman returned to her village after being trafficked to a large Chinese city to become a 'wife' for a rich elderly man. When he died, she was released and has returned to her village to help improve life and educate others about the dangers of trafficking.

We can take heart from the recent landmark judgement by the Court of Justice in West Africa, a place that remains one of slavery's strongholds. The Court in October 2008 ordered the Government of Niger to pay compensation to Hadijatou Mani for failing to protect her from slavery. At the age of twelve, Hadijatou had been sold, like hundreds of thousands of others in the region, to a master. The historic decision of the court was a strong message to other governments in the area that they must eradicate this evil in their midst – giving overdue hope at last to their citizens.

In the UK, too, there have been significant steps in the creation of the Human Trafficking Centre to improve coordination. This is linked to a national action plan to combat human trafficking in all its forms. We now need to see the political will and the commitment of the police and other authorities, both in time and resources, to use the weapons now at their disposal.

But we also have to step up our efforts to tackle global poverty and conflict as well as the prejudice and practices that prevent women playing their full role in society, thus helping provide the climate in which traffickers can operate.

Our response to misery in our midst and to the shocking stories we have read must not simply be sympathy for the victim; it must be indignation that such evil still exists. It was indignation that fuelled Wilberforce and his fellow campaigners' long battle against the vested interests whose wealth depended upon enslaving fellow human beings.

The trans-Atlantic slave trade was abolished, as former UN Secretary General Kofi Annan said during the 200th anniversary celebrations, because thousands of people took personal responsibility for what was happening around them. Appealing for a similar campaign in the twenty-first century, he said:

'We must approach today's abuses in the same spirit – each of us seeking, not to blame somebody else, but to think what we can do to hasten their end.

There is no evil so entrenched that it cannot be eradicated. Inspired by the abolitionists of two centuries ago, let us fight against exploitation and oppression and stand up for freedom and human dignity.'

His rallying call should inspire us all.

KOFI ANNAN

OUR RESPONSE

Time and time again – as this book shows – it is the female voices we hear. Our response to the scale of this crime and the depth of its depravity in the twenty-first century should also not be despair but anger. We must show the same resilience and passion for our cause as William Wilberforce and his fellow campaigners. No matter how many disappointments and defeats they suffered – and there were many – they never gave up, never stopped campaigning, educating and changing attitudes.

We need to mobilize public opinion in all our countries to see that legislation – domestic and international – is enforced. Trafficking is not something that happens somewhere else. It is happening in every community, in our streets, on our doorsteps. We will succeed in rooting out this misery and menace only when we stand up to be counted. We will have succeeded only when the fight to end trafficking in our fellow human beings becomes a mass movement demanding change.

Sex workers who were rescued by Maiti Nepal now work the border checking for potential traffickers and their victims. Due to the open border for Indian and Nepalese people travelling back and forth, it is easy for traffickers to cross over with their victims.

BUILD A BETTER WORLD

This is exactly the goal of STOP THE TRAFFIK – a global movement rooted, above all, in community action – which I am proud to support. There could be no more fitting tribute to the brave campaigners of history or to the authors of the Universal Declaration of Human Rights than for you and I to step up our efforts to tackle trafficking and build a world in which everyone – men, women and children – is free, safe and has the chance to prosper.

CHERIE BLAIR

CHAPTER 3

LOOK

Trafficking happens all over the world, including where you live, in your back yard.

Mary Rogers lives in the UK. She never imagined that her daughter would be at risk of sexual exploitation and trafficking for sex to men or organized networks in other towns or cities. She was shocked to learn that even on her doorstep, pimps and traffickers are grooming girls for sexual exploitation.

A MOTHER'S STORY

Mary Rogers'* thirteen-year-old daughter was sexually exploited by a group of men. After she had been abducted by two of them, she finally agreed to testify to the police. Her mother tells her story.

'Jessica* was born with Ollier disease: a rare skeletal disorder that affects bone development. As she got older, it became more noticeable that one of her arms was shorter. "I feel really ugly, mum," she would sometimes say. "No lad I like is ever going to fancy me."

She wouldn't go out without a jacket, even if it was scorching. So I was really proud of her when she became a majorette. We travelled the country taking part in competitions, and one of my proudest moments was when her team won first prize at a holiday camp. My daughter couldn't have looked any happier.

Jessica was a normal teenager in every other way. She was sporty and bright and we never had any problems at school. At weekends she went out with her friends, but she was always in on time. Occasionally, I'd find out that she'd had a drop of cider or something, and she was grounded for a couple of nights, but you expect that.

One Friday night – July 2005 – she didn't come home. Jessica was thirteen. "See you," she'd called out as normal when she left. But 10 p.m. came and went. At 11.30 p.m., I started ringing round her friends. Shortly after, I rang the police. I rang my ex-husband too, and we went out looking for her.

That was probably the worst night of my life. We searched for her the whole of the next day, too. Then the police called. She'd been picked up with a friend called Gemma. Gemma was in foster care. A lot of the girls picked on her because she was scruffy. "I feel really sorry for her, mum," Jessica had said. "You don't have to be like the other girls," I'd replied. What I didn't know at that point was that Gemma was being groomed by a group of men.

I grounded Jessica for going missing. But the next day she was gone. Gemma was missing from her foster home, too. I rang the police again.

On Tuesday morning I got a knock on the front door. Two female police officers asked to come in. "We believe Jessica is being sexually exploited by a group of Asian men," they said.

Over the next few months, life became a nightmare. Jessica kept coming home with presents, like perfume, jewellery and mobile phones. She wouldn't tell me where she got them. "Do you like my gold chain, mum? Do you like my ring?" she'd say. And she was different. If I tried to keep her in, she'd find a way to get out. She'd tell me to "F-off" all the time.

Jessica was, by now, running wild at school, too. She got suspended twice. She didn't do any schoolwork for the whole of year nine. School just didn't exist for her any more. She'd just dump her uniform and run out; I don't remember how many times I bought a new one.

She was coming in with bruises and love bites all over her, too. She wasn't washing and didn't care about herself. Within three months, I literally didn't know her any more. We'd had a really good relationship, but she barely spoke to me now. "It's nothing to do with you, get out of my life. I don't care for you and I don't want you to care for me," she'd say. I told her: "You've got a problem then, because I will never stop caring for you."

Jessica became the number-one missing person in the county. I rang the police 90 times. That's how many times she went missing. I'd wait for them to arrive at all hours of the night. And I'd go to work on automatic pilot.

The police would find Jessica all over the place and in various towns. They would pick her up on grass verges, where she'd been dumped by these men and had fallen asleep. She was once left on the hard shoulder of a motorway. She had been drugged and passed around a group of men. She had absolutely no concept of who she was.

The men sent her into shops to pinch whiskey for them. As a result, Jessica and I went to court three times for shoplifting. Once, when Jessica was found lying drunk in the street, I was also fined by the police. She was fetched out of cells so many times at the police station. Then the police told me that they had found ecstasy tablets on her. This was the first I knew that she was definitely taking drugs.

The worst thing for a parent is not being able to control or protect your own daughter. It was so hard for me to sleep at night. How do you sleep when your thirteen-year-old is out on the streets somewhere, and you're not able to protect her? You question yourself: "Is it something I've done? Have I treated her any different to my other children?"

But then the police started telling me how the grooming process works. They said the lads involved have fast cars and are usually young and good-looking. They get the girls into the car by offering them a bit of vodka or something, some loud music and a bit of a drive. The girls may say "no" one night, but another night they might have had a bit of cider and say "yes". That's when it starts.

The girls get given alcohol and presents, especially mobile phones. They call the girls "princess" and make them feel special. Then it's a few spliffs, and, before they know it, they pass the girls on to older men. The older men introduce the girls to class A drugs. That's when the girls become reliant on them: the men and the drugs.

The girls are often called to come out at all times of the day and night, so it starts to cause problems within the family. That's the idea. The men are seen to be fun, so they're the good ones and the family are bad. The parents are made to look like they just want to keep the girl in, and make her life miserable. But it becomes more sinister because then it's payback time.

The drugs cost money, you see. They send the girls to pinch things. The girls are passed around. They might threaten to rape their mum and smash up their house if they don't do what they're told, or they go to the police.

For a long time, I couldn't understand why Jessica kept going back. But then I understood. It was the drugs. They started her off on weed, then ecstasy, then crack cocaine. That was Jessica's journey in zero to twelve months.

'They used to say, when they were giving Jessica drugs, that they were God; that they ruled; there was no escape.'

MARY ROGERS – JESSICA'S MUM

Sexually, I don't know what they have done to her. I have a good idea, because I saw some of the letters Gemma wrote to Jessica, saying what these men had done to her. The letters were absolutely filthy. So much so, that I couldn't read them all.

In our city, a specialist unit was set up to investigate cases of sexual exploitation. I just used to ring Sarah, the sexual exploitation officer, and pass her the letters. Whenever she tried to tell me details, I would say: "Stop. Don't tell me." I can't know the details. I don't think I could live if I knew them. I am just trying to survive.

At first, I didn't want anyone to know. I felt ashamed that she had got involved, because I blamed her at first. But after the police had been here about thirty times, I didn't feel shame any more. It wasn't about shame. It was about a young girl, a child, being exploited. I wanted these men caught. I wanted them locked up. But the law seemed powerless to protect my daughter. And nobody seemed to do anything.

In September 2005, I called social services. I begged them for help. I didn't want to put her in a foster home, but they basically said that's all they could do. They thought I needed some respite. I had two other children and I needed some rest from it all. Then they put her in a foster home round the corner. I hated it. In foster care, Jessica went from bad to worse. Every night I would get a text from her foster carer saying she wasn't home. So it was me out, again, looking for her. The foster carer didn't have the power to keep Jessica in. It was open the door and see you later.

"You've got to move her out of the county, before I find her dead in a gutter," I pleaded with social services. I believed that was where I was going to find her, because she kept getting more and more presents, more and more bruises, and more and more love bites.

I went to see my local MP at Christmas 2005. I became on first-name terms with his secretary because I rang every week saying that I wanted something done; that I wanted her moved out of the county. My MP wrote to social services, whom I was now ringing daily. I became a nuisance because I was totally desperate.

In the end, I went back to my MP. "My daughter's being dumped all over the place. If you don't do something about it, I'm going to put it in the papers," I said. Within weeks, social services had found her a place out of county.

She moved in January 2006 and went into therapeutic foster care. They have one child at a time and they do therapeutic work with the children. I couldn't have asked for a better placement.

But Jessica had only been there a week and a half when two men abducted her. One was forty-seven, the other aged thirty-one. Jessica was missing for a couple of days before she was found, with Gemma, walking along in the city. The police arrested the girls. My daughter alleges that she was hit by one of these men with an iron bar. I think that that pushed her to testify.

The sexual exploitation officer told me that Jessica wouldn't do what they told her to do. I put a stop to it there. The only way I can handle this is not to know the details. But sexual stuff obviously happened, because they were charged with a number of offences, including sex with a child under sixteen, detaining a child without lawful authority and supplying a class A drug. I'm scared what my actions will be if these men get let off. I am really afraid that I will go off my head.

I am 100% sure there were a lot more men, but I think these two have probably inflicted the worst physical, emotional and psychological damage on Jessica. I will never be able to get my head round it. Never. My whole outlook on life has changed. I am not happy. I'll never be happy again. I don't like the world. I feel I have been very naive about what's going on.

The guilt is terrible. You go right back to when they were born. I know she had low self-esteem because of her arm. Perhaps this made her more vulnerable to their flattery? Obviously, it was me who gave birth to her, so you blame yourself. It's only when people start talking to you that you realize these girls are victims of criminal acts: you are not to blame and they are not to blame. These men are to blame.

In the beginning, I didn't believe drugs could have had this kind of hold; that they could strip my daughter of who she was in every way. These men exploited her so that she needed these drugs. She was having to do these awful things to get drugs; all the while, they were passing her from pillar to post. She would literally get in anybody's car. That kills me.

Her relationship with her older sister does not exist any more. And my ten-year-old lad has become much more insecure. He used to go to his room and cry. 'I don't like it,' he'd say. I tried to hide things from him, but you can't always do that when things are happening under your own roof, and the police are coming round all the time. Jessica was very abusive to me and he's seen all that. She hit me sometimes, too, when I tried to drag her back through her bedroom window.

I feel I can't get involved in a relationship now. How can I put all this on somebody? I can't. That's how I see it. This is what my life revolves around now. I don't go out much. I read a lot, to try to understand what's ahead for us; to understand how to help Jessica deal with all that's gone on.

I have felt very alone. Because my mum was poorly, I chose not to tell her. She died recently. It was very hard not being able to talk to her. And Jessica's dad couldn't handle what was going on, so he went off the scene for a while. He has come back on board now.

A lot of people think things like this only happens to "bad" families. But it can happen to anybody. You wonder how you can have a daughter who's so happy one minute, and who's drugged up and has no respect for anybody the next. But it happens.

Now, when she comes to visit from foster care, she needs a drink to face people. She's got problems in her head – big ones. When she has had a drink, she threatens to kill herself. "Mum you don't know what it's like. Being sexually abused is the worst thing ever. I just don't want to be here, life is not worth living," she said to me, once.

I asked her dad to stay one night because I was frightened she would do something. She was singing nursery rhymes and getting all the stuff out from when she was little. She had her majorette's medal round her neck. "I want to die with this medal on. It was the favourite time of my life," she said.

Sarah says to me that the girls don't want to have sex with these men. Looking at her, I can't even believe that she has. She is just a little girl. These men have taken her innocence and her childhood. They have taken away mine, and all my children's normal way of life.

Jessica had hundreds of numbers on her phone. In fact, she had all different SIM cards and all different phones. I have given them to the police, so I don't understand why they can't prosecute. But the police say that there are so many loopholes in the law.

We've got a law that says sex with someone under sixteen is not allowed. But prosecution relies on the testimony of the child in a court of law. In practice, when a child is over thirteen she will have to testify. The men know that. They groom the girls so that they can have sex with them as soon as they turn thirteen. The girls are often too frightened to give evidence, or they don't always fully understand that they were groomed, and that these men weren't real boyfriends.

my daughter used to say, 'I told them I was seventeen', and I hadn't even asked her a question. So you can see right away it's drummed into them. That's how I knew she'd been told to say that.

Jessica also said many times: "Mum, don't mess about. They'll come round here with baseball bats." You start to believe it yourself. I've wanted to get in my car and go round and kill them. But then I think: I've got two other children and what would that do?

I've been involved in telling my story to social services, the police and government bodies. Often, people are open-mouthed. **This is happening on our doorstep** and some of them haven't got a bloody clue. It means that parents like me, and the girls, often don't get the help, services, support, or understanding that we need.

I want to put a stop to this for other parents and other kids. That's why I'm speaking out. Nobody warned me about sexual exploitation, nobody warned me that there are lads who drive round in their posh cars and loud music, and try to groom girls. I didn't warn my daughter. I want other parents to be aware. These men do it because they can. They can get away with it.

I have three children, not two. But I have only had two children for the last couple of years. And I'll never get my daughter back. Not the daughter I had. All I can do now is try to get her back on track as much as I can. '

AS TOLD TO CHRISTINE MILES

An extract from *STOP! She's my daughter* — where mothers of abuse victims share their stories of grooming and child sexual exploitation in the UK — published by CROP (Coalition for the Removal of Pimping) © Christine Miles

The two men who abducted Jessica pleaded guilty to charges of sex with a child under sixteen, detaining a child without lawful authority, and supplying a class A drug. The accused were sentenced to imprisonments of five years and eight months each. With dependency issues remaining, Jessica remains a vulnerable target. Her family continues to struggle with the long-term impact sexual exploitation has had on Jessica and themselves.

* Names have been changed.

CROP is a national charity working with parents and carers to end the sexual exploitation of children and young people by pimps and traffickers. For more information on its work, visit www.crop1.org.uk; email: info@cropuk.org.uk; telephone: UK +44 (0)113 2403040.

'In addition to children being trafficked into the UK from abroad, British national children or young people can also be victims of trafficking within the UK. This is often identified in situations where the victims are moved from one location to another irrespective of distance. This may actually be within a town or between towns and cities in the UK, very often for the purposes of sexual exploitation.

These young victims are passed between groups of men for the purpose of being sexually assaulted and raped by them and others in their network. This is a serious, organised crime.'

INTERNAL TRAFFICKING – WHAT IS IT?

Jessica is not alone. Andy Baker, Deputy Director of the Serious Organised Crime Agency (SOCA) in the UK, writes:

'Initiatives like STOP THE TRAFFIK are tackling head on the issues of organized immigration crime and trafficking in human beings as well as the associated exploitation, extreme violence and misery inflicted on victims. It is important that society does not turn a blind eye to this issue – it can be happening on the street where you live, work or socialize; whether that is in a source, transit or destination country. It is equally important that we engage in the widest appropriate partnerships in order to reduce the harm caused.

The harm caused to victims can be difficult to imagine but may include long-term economic bondage, perpetual fear, violence and even rape or murder. Likewise, harm can be caused to the victim's immediate family or friends and to the communities where they come from or to those communities where they are destined to be exploited.

Recent work on Operation Pentameter II, a UK police operation, exposed trafficking for sexual exploitation, and specifically identified source countries of China and others in South-East Asia as well as Eastern Europe, although the issue is not restricted to those countries alone. Women, children and men can be openly duped; they may be told that they will receive legal employment or just a better life. In some instances families give up their loved ones for money or because they wrongly believe they will have a better life. This deception or coercion may well imprison the victim in a life of misery – forever!

Law enforcement agencies across the world are focusing on this ongoing tragedy and need the help of friends, neighbours and people in agencies that provide support. Don't turn a blind eye – bring it to attention – anything will help. You will certainly stop someone being harmed and could save a life.'

Traffickers used friends of these girls, who had already been trafficked, to try and persuade them to leave the village. The girls refused but remain vulnerable to trafficking in the area.

Hundreds of thousands of other young girls are subjected to the same kinds of horrific abuse around the world. Andrea, a young woman in Colombia, described her ordeal to the UNODC:

ANDREA'S STORY

'At that moment, my nightmare began. I was terrified when they showed me what I was expected to do – I felt I just couldn't do it. I've been through many things, but never something like that, so I told them that I wasn't going to and that I was going back home. I was shocked when they told me that wasn't possible – they said they had invested a lot of money in me, and I had to work to pay them back, because I now belonged to the network. I thought about escaping, but I was afraid of being physically hurt or killed. I worked hard for six months, but they have no mercy on you… they're just demeaning. During this time, I was sold many times, and this happened every ten days – sometimes I just didn't know where I was. You're like a commodity to them.'

ANDREA FERNANDA, INTERVIEWED BY THE UNODC COUNTRY OFFICE IN COLOMBIA, PUBLISHED IN UN, 2008, *HUMAN TRAFFICKING: AN OVERVIEW.*

Those who escape are often re-trafficked. Their traffickers track them down, or the women themselves find no alternative but to return. Social worker Hannah Wilson has worked to support trafficked women in Albania with BMS World Mission.

HANNAH'S STORY

'I've seen people suffer and be treated badly, and seen people re-trafficked and go back into it because they feel they've got nothing else and no other way to survive. They think they are worthless. I've also seen it's very difficult to get a job if you've been in prostitution. There is a prejudice towards them. I'd love for us to help these women believe in themselves again.'

Europe's sex industry is booming, and traffickers are reaping the benefits. Trafficked people need to be protected, to be given back what should never have been taken away: safety, hope and choice. The UK government Joint Committee On Human Rights 26th Report recently stated: 'What we have tried to do is look at the scale of the sex industry and that gives you a reasonable picture of what is likely to happen in terms of women being trafficked in for that industry. Recently we did some work looking at the sex industry and we saw about 264,000 men spending at least £6.6 million per year on saunas, flats, et cetera. That was taken from some work through Punternet, where men talk about their experience of buying sex. Certainly we are finding that the sex industry is expanding in lap dancing, limousine services, takeaway services, and as long as you have got that expansion you are likely to have women trafficked in to fulfil those services.' (*www.publications.parliament.uk/pa/jt200506/jtselect/jtrights/245/24507.htm.*)

Bangkok bar signs. *A girl working in Germany.*

TRANS-NATIONAL TRAFFICKING
The facts

◢ Approximately 80% of the estimated 600,000 to 800,000 trans-national trafficking victims per year – or some 640,000 – are women and girls.

US Department of State –
Trafficking in Persons (TIP) Report, 2007

◢ Trafficking is mostly trans-national – but sex trafficking also occurs within countries.

UNODC

WOMEN AND TRAFFICKING
The facts

◢ 70% of all women who are trafficked are sexually exploited.

US Department of State

◢ 98% of those trafficked into sexual exploitation are women and girls.

International Labour Organization (ILO)

◢ 70% of these women met the criteria for post-traumatic stress disorder in the same range as treatment-seeking combat veterans and victims of state-organized torture.

– 'Human Trafficking and Development: the Role of Microfinance' in
Transformation, Vol.23, 3 July 2006

◢ Trafficking into the sex trade remains the most common form of trafficking.

UNODC

ECONOMIC EXPLOITATION

Traffickers exploit need. The people they prey on are those struggling with poverty, desperate to improve their lot in life. Often, it is the women and girls who are lured into the sex trade with empty promises of money and travel, of well-paid jobs as cleaners, au pairs, waitresses, bartenders or models. In West Africa, for example, it is the children of the poor, especially boys, who are drawn into the cocoa plantations of the Ivory Coast (Côte d'Ivoire) with empty promises of food and money (see Chapter 5, BUY). Before they know it, these people – people with the same hopes, needs and dreams as us – have been trapped, sold, shipped off and forced into a life of unimaginable humiliation and suffering.

HOW DO THEY DO IT?

Traffickers use a number of different means to recruit their victims: individual recruiters might hang out in bars and clubs looking out for interested people, sham agencies offer work or study abroad, or it can be as simple as placing an ad in the local paper. Which is exactly what the traffickers do.

BRENDA'S STORY

My name is Brenda. It took me some time to realize who I was and what my name was. The reason for that is it was just too painful to be me so if I became someone else I didn't have to recognize the pain Brenda was going through.

Adverts stuck to trees in Cisinau, Moldova.

Some women are forced to become domestic slaves.

I was born in Chicago, USA to a fifteen-year-old girl named Ernestine. She died six months later and I was left in the care of my grandmother. They would take advantage of me when she was drinking. The earliest I can remember of being molested is when I was four or five years old. By the time I was nine I had become numb to the abuse and had decided to become a prostitute. I saw prostitutes working in front of my grandma's house out the window and to me they looked shiny. All I ever wanted to be was shiny but the molestation had taken that shine away from me. So I promised myself that I would make them pay for it that way.

When I was fifteen I was working near the Gold Coast. During the twenty-five years that I worked as a prostitute I was taken to many different places and cities and states, even outside of America. My first experience of travelling without permission was one night when two pimps pulled up while I was coming out of a hotel. One got out and told me I was under pimp arrest as I began to struggle. He grabbed me while the other man got out the car, unlocked his trunk and threw me in.When they opened the trunk, I was met with a large stick. I thought I was going to die. They told me that they would now represent me. If I didn't work for them they saw no reason to keep me alive. I worked for these two creeps for a month and then they picked up another girl the same way.

I escaped after six months. I was terrified whenever I saw a car that even looked close to the car I was thrown in. I started working in massage parlours to feel safer and to have some security from the pimps on the street. I soon found out the massage parlours and strip clubs had their own kind of pimps – the ones who hide behind the desk and say they're employers. I didn't mind that I had to give a percentage of my money to the establishment and that I wasn't allowed to leave the premises when I was on call. What did disturb me was the way they moved us around like cattle. You never knew where you would end up. It was also normal to wake up and find the girl next to you was gone. You knew not to ask where she was or give any information that you knew she was there.

The last I dealt with that organization was 1982 in New Orleans. I ran away with a guy to California. I was still involved in prostitution but just at street level. The first time I wanted to stop was after I had a baby. I was referred to The Salvation Army. I stayed there, got clean and came back home to Chicago. After a year I relapsed and started working the streets again. That was in 1994 and I worked the streets till 1997.

Trafficking can be occur internationally or or even right here in the USA; right here in our own back yards. As an advocate I see and hear of trafficking happening in our everyday communities with our young women and girls. It doesn't have to be done across the borders. It can happen across a state line or a community line. If a person takes a women from point A to B with the intent of prostituting her body it is trafficking.

THE SALVATION ARMY 'PROMISE' (PARTNERSHIP TO RESCUE
OUR MINORS FROM SEXUAL EXPLOITATION) PROGRAM

NOI'S STORY

Noi, a slender, petite girl from Thailand, was recruited through an 'agency'.

Noi grew up in a foster family in rural Thailand. But instead of the comforting home she had hoped for, the foster home was a place of continued rape and sexual abuse. At fifteen, seeking to escape these abuses, Noi found a foreign labour agent in Bangkok who advertised well-paid waitress jobs in Japan.

She flew to Japan and later learned that she had entered Japan on a tourist visa under a false identity. On her arrival in Japan, she was taken to a karaoke bar where the owner raped her, subjected her to a blood test and then bought her.

'I felt like a piece of flesh being inspected,' she recounted. The brothel madam told Noi that she had to pay off a large debt for her travel expenses. She was warned that girls who tried to escape were brought back by the Japanese mafia, severely beaten, and their debts doubled. The only way to pay off the debt was to see as many clients as quickly as possible.

Some clients beat the girls with sticks, belts and chains until they bled. If the victims returned crying, they were beaten by the madam and told that they must have provoked the client. The prostitutes routinely used drugs before sex 'so that we didn't feel so much pain.' Most clients refused to use condoms. The girls were given pills to avoid pregnancy and pregnancies were terminated with home abortions.

Women on a break at a bar in Bangkok.

Even for those few girls who managed to pay off their debt and work independently, the ordeal was not over. Usually they were arrested by the police before being deported. Noi finally managed to escape with the help of a Japanese national governmental organization (NGO).

Traffickers also go as far as to exploit the trust of informal networks of friends or relatives, even entering into false marriages.

US DEPARTMENT OF STATE TRAFFICKING
IN PERSONS REPORT,
JUNE 2004

NEARY'S STORY

Neary grew up in rural Cambodia. Her parents died when she was a child, and, in an effort to give her a better life, her sister married her off when she was seventeen. Like so many trafficked people, Neary also thought she was starting a new chapter in her life and that things were looking up. Neither of the girls suspected that Neary's marriage was a sham, and that her days were numbered.

Three months later, Neary and her husband went to visit a fishing village. Her husband rented a room in what Neary thought was a guest-house. She had been looking forward to it – it would be like a honeymoon, a break from the monotonous slog of her everyday life.

But when Neary woke the next morning, her husband was gone. The owner of the house told her she had been sold by her husband for $300 and that she was actually in a brothel.

For five years, Neary was raped by five to seven men every day. In addition to brutal physical abuse, Neary was infected with HIV and contracted AIDS. The brothel threw her out when she became sick, and she eventually found her way to a local shelter. She died of HIV/AIDS at the age of twenty-three.

Brothel in Cambodia.

Newspaper ads, agencies and false marriages are just some of the devices used by traffickers to 'recruit'. Now, with increased use of the Internet and highly sophisticated organization, this crime is becoming harder to detect. Traffickers have become masters of disguise, rotating victims to avoid identification, doing business from discreet apartments, escort agencies and massage parlours rather than brothels.

Now most trafficking occurs through what people like to call discreet apartments and escort agencies.

WWW.STATE.GOV/G/TIP/C16482.HTM

TRANS-NATIONAL TRAFFICKING
Sex tourism

In some countries the demand for trafficked young women and children is fuelled by sex tourism. Sex tourism is rife in Cambodia, Thailand, Costa Rica, Mexico and Brazil, but is also associated with a number of other countries around the world.

Poipet in Cambodia is known among tour guides as the 'Wild West' of South-East Asia, on account of its roaring sex trade and gambling scene. It is estimated that one-third of the prostitutes in Cambodia are children, and people go there to buy or abduct children. Girls as young as five are trafficked over the border into Thailand.

SOKHA AND MAKARA'S STORY

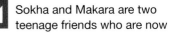

Sokha and Makara are two teenage friends who are now able to giggle together like any other girls their age. But it hasn't always been this way. Their childhood has been filled with pain, and only now are they beginning to feel hope again.

These girls were sold to a trafficker, who promised them good jobs in Thailand. When they were sold, they were fourteen and fifteen years old.

Sokha explains that her mother was ill with a liver complaint. The family needed money to pay for drugs to treat her, and they also hoped to buy some land to build a home. But, reality turned out to be very different. There were no 'good jobs' for the girls, Sokha's mother died within a year, and the family couldn't afford to buy land.

Sokha, now seventeen, says, 'I felt cheated. The traffickers used us for slave jobs, and whilst they earned lots of money we only got enough to feed ourselves each day.' She explains how she and Makara, now sixteen, were given jobs selling fruit, but it did not pay enough. Soon, their bosses forced them into sleeping with men to pay their way – the latest victims of sex tourism.

A partner of the international charity, Tearfund, provides young girls with sewing skills, counselling and the loving support of a local church. The girls' parents met staff from Tearfund's partner, Cambodian Hope Organization (CHO), and gave them photos to pass on to an organization in Thailand that rescues girls from prostitution. It found – and duly rescued – Sokha and Makara.

By then, the girls' ordeal had been going on for nearly a year. Sokha says, 'It's good to be home. We are grateful to CHO who have brought us back to our home, provided us with counselling, taught us the skill of sewing, and brought us into the church.' When asked what they hope for in the future, Sokha says she hopes to set up her own sewing business and employ and help girls in her situation.

'We were scared all the time in Thailand,' she says. 'Now I'm happy, getting support, living with my family and free to work when I want.'

TEARFUND

Sokha and Makara were rescued, but their ordeal – being trafficked and abused as children – is endured by thousands of others like them. Sex tourists, often from the West, travel to developing countries, expecting easily accessible, low-cost sex with children.

FROM LEFT TO RIGHT: *A former brothel in Cambodia has become AIM 4 Asia's new community centre in Svay Pak, for survivors of sexual exploitation.*

Girl's view of a man approaching her room in Svay Pak.

A tiny room where the girls were held prisoner in Svay Pak.

Poem from one of the girls' rooms in Svay Pak.

It is a deeply uncomfortable thought. Unthinkable. But we must think about it – it is a reality in every part of the world. And it is only as people think about it, face up to it and speak out that that reality will be changed.

Svay Pak in Cambodia is one of many thriving destinations for the sexual trafficking of children, its numerous brothels packed with primary-school aged girls. It is a hot spot for the sexual trafficking of children and young women throughout Cambodia and Thailand, as well as a venue for the production of child pornography.

On the wall of one of the brothels is a poem written by a trafficked girl. Here is a translation. It is full of melancholy resignation; weariness at what this girl feels is the futility of her own existence. This is a despair she should never have known, a despair that needs to be replaced: by safety, hope and choice.

There is a happy time, and then it ends
There is love, but for a short time and only in front of my face
Men boast we are pretty, but they are not honest with us
We boast we are pretty while we wear make up
No one knows it, but we are like petals falling from a flower
The only beauty we have is spiritual
Life is just life, it has no meaning

In response to the horrifying truth of child trafficking, countries in the West have passed laws making it a crime to sexually abuse a child in another country. But making something illegal doesn't always stop it happening. Despite being outlawed throughout the world, trafficking is still growing fast, and the laws of the West do little in the countries of the East. Urgent action is needed. There is more information at: www.worldvision.org/get_involved.nsf/child/globalissues_stp.

One of the main organizations fighting trafficking into the sex trade is End Child Prostitution, Child Pornography and the Trafficking of Children for Sexual Purposes (ECPAT). To learn how you can support their campaign, visit: www.ecpat.net.

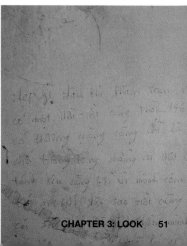

It is important to inform ourselves, to raise awareness and to speak out. These women and children may not have a voice. But we do.

> **'It is an evil time when the world is dumb before injustice. When the oppressed, the poor, the deprived, cry aloud unto heaven, while the judges and the lords of the Earth keep silent...**
>
> **...[These people] who feel pain and sorrow like you, to whom violence is done; who have joys and hopes like you; who feel honour and insult like you... your brothers and sisters! "Are you dumb?" O no, you are not dumb, your voice is heard, loud and clear on Earth!'**
>
> **DIETRICH BONHOEFFER (1906–45)**

Trafficking and sexual exploitation go hand in hand. But it isn't only the sex industry that promotes the trafficking of persons.

CHILD SOLDIERS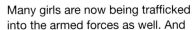

Many girls are now being trafficked into the armed forces as well. And there, sexual abuse is a constant threat, in addition to the danger from the violence of conflict.

In Northern Uganda, the Lord's Resistance Army (LRA) has been conducting a campaign of violence and terror for about twenty years. During that time they have abducted more than 20,000 children, using them as soldiers and as sex slaves. Once conscripted, children as young as ten are forced to commit atrocities against their families, as part of a ritual designed to bind a terrible loyalty through guilt and fear.

The use of child soldiers is a problem far beyond Uganda. It is estimated that there are 300,000 child soldiers around the world involved in conflicts in around thirty countries (for further information, visit: www.un.org/special-rep/children-armed-conflict/English/Overview.html).

'When you're a kid, it's easy to be deceived. Each Sunday when I walked down from the town, where my mum had a business, they would urge me to go with them, telling me that I would have a really good time, that it was better to go with them than to keep on working.

On my twelfth birthday, they came back for me. My mum was away at work, so I took the chance and escaped with them... Five months later I regretted being there, but there was no chance of leaving.

Besides, they told my mum that I was dead, that they had already killed me… just like what happened to my cousin who went with the [military], and when she tried to escape, they caught her, sent her to the war council, and executed her. I had been on the fortieth front for two months when I got wounded. It was very hard. I was… in the middle of a combat situation, and I had to assemble a bomb to throw at the army, but I grabbed it with the wrong hand. The soldiers were burning me [shooting too close] and I changed the bomb from one hand to another, and it exploded and blew my leg off… In that moment I felt blood coming out of me, very fast, and I screamed when I saw it. I was legless. I screamed again, and then a guy… grabbed me, but I fainted… We surrendered on 20 July. We were very afraid because they warned us that the only thing we couldn't do was to let ourselves get caught alive, or surrender to the military, because the first thing they would do to women was raping and torturing us, penetrate us with a wooden stick and then kill us… Now my dream is that they help me to get back my leg, so I can walk again. After that I'd like to go to high school and then to the nursery school… I'd like that.'

XIMENA, INTERVIEWED BY THE UNODC COUNTRY OFFICE IN COLOMBIA,
PUBLISHED IN UN, 2008 *HUMAN TRAFFICKING: AN OVERVIEW*

WOMEN AND TRAFFICKING
Women's war zone

◢ Young women make up about 30% of the estimated 300,000 child soldiers today

◢ One in five countries have used girl soldiers in armed conflict in the last two decades

◢ Girls and young women are especially affected by war and conflict: they are sexually abused and raped as a tactic to humiliate and destroy the opponent's culture and population.

PLAN INTERNATIONAL
(www.plan-international.org/news/girls_war_report)

FORCED LABOUR

Men and women are being trafficked into a range of industries and forced to work as slaves. They might work on a building site, they might be beggars. As with the sex trade, traffickers use the simplest methods to spin a web of lies, of coercing people into compliance.

LABOUR TRAFFICKING
Trafficking into forced labour

Using force, fraud or coercion to recruit, harbor, transport, obtain or employ a person for labour or services in involuntary servitude, peonage, debt bondage or slavery. This is found in:

- ◢ Domestic situations (nannies or maids)
- ◢ Cleaning services
- ◢ Sweatshop factories
- ◢ Janitorial jobs
- ◢ Construction
- ◢ Agricultural/farm work
- ◢ Restaurants and bars
- ◢ Hotels
- ◢ Panhandling (begging)

TVPA

ORGAN TRAFFICKING

When you consider that right now in the US alone there are over 50,000 people awaiting organ transplants, it becomes clear that there is money to be made by the ruthless for the trafficking of human organs. The needs are being met by the world's poorest people, some of whom are selling a kidney for as little as $1,000 in order to provide for their basic necessities, while the brokers of this trade are taking home upwards of $200,000 for arranging a transplant for their client.

India criminalized organ sales in 1994, but not without making allowances for 'unrelated kidney sales'. Between 1984 and 1988, 130 patients from the United Arab Emirates purchased new kidneys from living persons for a price ranging between 2,600 US$ and 3,300 US$, while a commission in Pernambuco state, Brazil, discovered that thirty Brazilians had sold kidneys to the same organ trafficking ring, which were then transported to Durban, South Africa for operations paid for by mostly Israeli customers. It is truly an international trade. One man in the state even placed an ad in a local newspaper that read: 'I am willing to sell any organ of my body that is not vital to my survival and that could help save another person's life in exchange for an amount of money that will allow me to feed my family.' Brazil has recently passed laws that make every one of its citizens automatically an eligible organ donor, unless they choose to opt out.

In some cases, organ traffickers take not just their body parts, but their lives. In 1995 Moses Mokgethi was sentenced in the Rand Supreme Court, Guateng, South Africa to life imprisonment for the murder of six children between the ages of four and nine whose bodies were harvested for their hearts, livers and other body parts, then sold to a local township businessman. Nancy Sheper-Hughes, head of the Organs Watch project, has called it 'the New Cannibalism'.

Around the world trafficking is on the increase, from trafficking for the purpose of sexual exploitation to the trafficking of organs. In response to this a number of anti-trafficking laws have been passed, both internationally and nationally.

HUMAN TRAFFICKING: INTERNATIONAL MEASURES
AGAINST TRAFFICKING THE UNITED NATIONS

GLOBAL RESPONSE
International action

◢ Slavery has long been prohibited by Article 4 of the 1948 Universal Declaration of Human Rights: 'No one shall be held in slavery or servitude; slavery and the slave trade shall be prohibited in all their forms.'

◢ There is also the 1989 UN Convention on the Rights of the Child, which prohibits child trafficking in Article 35: 'Prevent the abduction of, the sale of or traffic in children for any purpose or in any form.'

◢ However, it is only relatively recently that there has been an international stand against all forms of human trafficking. The 2000 UN Protocol to Prevent, Suppress and Punish Trafficking in Persons, otherwise known as the 'Palermo Protocol', set an internationally agreed definition of human trafficking, the dislocation of someone by deception or coercion for exploitation, and identified the key areas of general prevention, prosecution of traffickers, and protection of victims.

◢ The Millennium Declaration was also agreed in 2000, which committed UN member states to achieving eight Millennium Development Goals by 2015. The goals address poverty, lack of education, gender inequality, child mortality, maternal mortality, HIV/AIDS, environmental degradation, and global cooperation. These factors make people vulnerable to human trafficking.

COUNCIL OF EUROPE CONVENTION

Esther Benjamins Trust's EBT Retrieval teams regularly visit circuses to rescue trafficked children, upon returning the children to safety they reunite them with their families and provide long term support.

The 2005 Council of Europe Convention on Action against Trafficking in Human Beings is the regional implementation of the 2000 UN Protocol. It establishes minimum standards of protection for victims, including a thirty-day reflection and recovery period, free from the threat of removal from the country they end up in, and with access to support services such as housing, healthcare, translation, counselling, and other help. There are also set standards of criminal sanctions for traffickers and awareness and reduction efforts to prevent trafficking.

2000 UN PROTOCOL
Standards of Protection

◢   **It is the first international, legally-binding treaty that affirms human trafficking is a violation of human rights and which tries to safeguard these rights.**
◢   **Whilst many countries have signed and ratified the Convention, few have effectively implemented it, and it is only when local residents be the change they want to see in their communities that the traffic will be stopped.**

THE INTERNATIONAL LABOUR ORGANIZATION (ILO)

There have been various conventions by the ILO related to human trafficking. One of these is the 1999 ILO Convention 182, Article 3 of which addresses 'all forms of slavery or practices similar to slavery, such as the sale and trafficking of children, debt bondage and serfdom and forced or compulsory labour, including forced or compulsory recruitment of children for use in armed conflict'.

But what do these measures mean for the people being trafficked every day? Despite the laws in place, the very nature of trafficking – the vulnerability of those trafficked and the hidden nature of the crime – means that actually implementing the law is not as simple. In countries where police corruption is rife, those being trafficked find it almost impossible to trust the authorities. Often those who have been trafficked live in fear of being caught by their traffickers, and mistrust the

police. But the more we raise awareness of the crime of human trafficking, the harder it will be to ignore. The STOP THE TRAFFIK campaign aims to get ordinary people to increase awareness globally around the issue of people trafficking.

Children on the Edge's focus in Moldova is children and young people affected by trafficking, children with special needs and vulnerable children in poor rural communities, who are more at risk of exploitation and abuse due to poverty.

Traffickers are hard to identify, as they often go back to the village they came from and target people they know from their communities. One country where this is commonplace is Moldova.

'Moldova is the poorest country in Europe. Many in the countryside can only support their families by working abroad. Those left behind are easy prey for drug dealers and people traffickers.'

MICHAEL PALIN
FROM MICHAEL PALIN'S *NEW EUROPE,* 'WILD EAST', BBC, 2008

For his BBC series *New Europe*, Michael Palin visited Moldova, where a member of UNICEF, Tatiana, showed him a play put on by local children warning of the dangers of trafficking. This is a fine example of the work being done to raise awareness about trafficking, especially amongst young people.

Tatiana explained that traffickers are often people who have lived in the same village for twenty years. They go abroad, perhaps they are trafficked themselves, and then they become the traffickers. These traffickers then go back to their home town, where they are trusted, and recruit people they have known all their lives.

A woman begging for money in Cisinau, Moldova.

The children in the play enact how traffickers often drug their victims, who may then be trapped for years. Tatiana explained that about half the children performing this play have parents abroad. So for them trafficking is a very real issue. But this raising of awareness is limited in its effectiveness. It helps people to ask questions, but does little to change their situations.

When approached by a trusted member of their village with the temptation of money and a better life abroad, people remain susceptible to the crime of trafficking. More guidelines are needed on how people who choose to migrate can do so safely.

ANA'S STORY

Ana's story is typical of how easily Moldovan girls are being trafficked. She is seventeen and lives in a village in rural Moldova.

It is in the rural areas of Moldova that poverty is most evident. Houses are still patched together with mud and straw, water is drawn from the local wells and the only work available is poorly paid farming. The rural areas are also where there is the greatest risk of trafficking.

For Ana, this risk became a reality.

Having finished school a year earlier, Ana, faced with no real job prospects, decided she wanted to leave Moldova. An opportunity came up for her and a friend to go and work as waitresses overseas. They both literally jumped in the car straight away. Ana knew the people she was going with, so she trusted that the offer was legitimate.

She found out very quickly that it wasn't.

Ana at home with her sister.

Fortunately, when Ana failed to return home, her mother was immediately worried and contacted the local head teacher and police officer. The village is a very strong community and its response was swift.

Ana was lucky to be rescued – but she and others in her village are still at risk.

The issue is a complex mix in which economic migration, poverty, education and culture all combine to create a situation that involves families eroding and children increasingly vulnerable to the many evils, especially trafficking.

Children on the Edge is a charity working in Ana's village, where its strong community spirit is proving to be an ideal foundation for a coordinated community-led response. They are establishing a child and community centre in the heart of the village. Children come after school and can access learning support, nutrition and play activities, all designed to reinforce family and community structures.

There is no quick fix solution, but a grassroots community-led project that works directly with Ana and others in the village is the key to long-term change.

To learn more about the work of Children on the Edge, visit: www.childrenontheedge.org.

Girls such as Ana deserve to live knowing they are safe, that they have hope, and that they have the right to choose.

And there is hope. There are now stories that end with escape for those who have been trafficked – and prosecution for traffickers.

BIRGIT'S STORY

Birgit escaped her traffickers, who have been prosecuted. Birgit is now a confident young woman, impeccably dressed with dyed, straightened hair and lots of eyeliner. But her confidence today belies her traumatic childhood.

Birgit was only eleven when she was sold by her mother to a trafficker. Her trafficker brought her to the US, where she was locked in a house, cleaning, cooking and acting as a sex-slave to the trafficker and his family. Birgit became a teenage mother, and was severely scarred physically and psychologically by her experiences. But she escaped and reported her traffickers.

Today her traffickers are in prison and Birgit is free to pursue her life. With loving carers, as well as the prosecutors, advocates and law enforcers who took action, she has broken the chains of slavery.

After a long struggle, Birgit can now view herself not as a victim but a survivor. (http://stophumantrafficking.org.news.htm.)

UN: *HUMAN TRAFFICKING: AN OVERVIEW*

HUMAN TRAFFICKING
Common recruitment methods

- Individual recruiters looking for interested males and females in bars, cafés, clubs, discos and other public places
- Recruitment via informal networks of families and/or friends
- Advertisements offering work or study abroad
- Agencies offering work, study, marriage or travel abroad
- False marriages
- Purchase of children from their guardians.

MEANS OF RECRUITMENT:
- Complete coercion through abduction or kidnapping
- Selling a person, typically a child
- Deception by promises of legitimate employment and/or entry
- Deception through half-truths
- Deception about working conditions
- Abuse of vulnerability.

METHODS OF ENTRY TO THE TRANSIT/DESTINATION COUNTRY:
- Smuggled entry in vehicles, containers, trains, ferries or on foot
- By presentation of stolen or forged documents that provide a right of entry
- By presentation of bona-fide documents that provide false visa entitlements to enter or are fully legitimate.

FORMS OF EXPLOITATION:
- Forced labour
- Sexual exploitation
- Removal of organs and of body parts
- Criminal activities
- Begging
- Forced marriage
- Illicit adoption
- Exploitation in the army
- Armed conflicts.

FORMS OF CONTROL INCLUDE:
- Debt bondage
- Isolation by removal of identification and/or travel documents
- Linguistic and social isolation
- Violence and fear
- Threats of reprisals against the victim's family
- Psychological – imprisonment and torture
- Magical beliefs and practices.

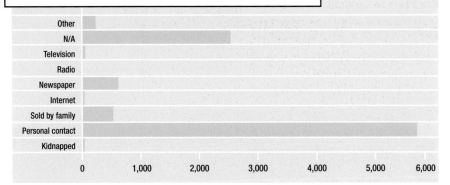

NUMBER OF VICTIMS BY RECRUITMENT METHOD

(Chart categories, top to bottom: Other, N/A, Television, Radio, Newspaper, Internet, Sold by family, Personal contact, Kidnapped)

Axis: 0, 1,000, 2,000, 3,000, 4,000, 5,000, 6,000

VICTIM PROFILES IN UNITED STATES GOVERNMENT, ILO, UNODC and IOM databases

	UNITED STATES GOVERNMENT	INTERNATIONAL LABOUR ORGANIZATION	UNITED NATIONS OFFICE ON DRUGS AND CRIME	INTERNATIONAL ORGANIZATION FOR MIGRATION
MAIN FOCUS	Global estimate of victims	Global estimate of victims	Country and regional patterns of international trafficking	Actual victims assisted by IOM in 78 countries
NUMBER OF VICTIMS	Some 600,000–800,000 people trafficked across borders in 2003 (estimate)	At least 2.45 million people trafficked internationally and internally between 1995 and 2004 (estimate)	N/A	7,711 victims assisted from 1999 to 2005
TYPE OF EXPLOITATION (PERCENTAGE)				
Commercial sex	55	43	87	81
Economic or forced labour	34	32	28	14
Mixed and other		25		5
GENDER AND AGE OF VICTIMS (PERCENTAGE)	80 female 50 minors	80 female 50 minors	71 female 2 male 44 children	83 female 15 male 2 not identified 13 minors
DEFINITION OF TRAFFICKING USED	TVPA 2000	Trafficking Protocol	Trafficking Protocol	Trafficking Protocol
CRITERIA FOR DATA COLLECTION	Trans-national trafficking	Internal and trans national trafficking	Trans-national trafficking	Internal and trans-national trafficking

SOURCE: United States of America, Government Accountability Office, *Human Trafficking: Better Data, Strategy, and Reporting Needed to Enhance U.S Anti-trafficking Efforts Abroad*. GAO Report GAO-06-825 (July 2006).

BEYOND THE STATISTICS

 Now you begin to have a picture of what trafficking looks like. But we need to look further.

Look beyond the statistics. See through the eyes of the people being trafficked every day. Look into those eyes and understand their pain.

If those eyes looked back at us, what would they see? Apathetic pity? Sympathy, but no action? Or determination to make a difference?

We need not just sight, but vision.

> 'Master master worked the slave
> Who ran for liberty,
> The master made us perm and shave
> Come children see.
>
> If slave drivers be men of words
> We curse that poetry,
> Its roots you'll find are so absurd
> Come children see.
>
> ...Fear not his science or his gun
> Just know what you can be,
> And children we shall overcome
> Come children see.'

FROM 'MASTER', BY BENJAMIN ZEPHANIAH, featured in *Unheard Voices*, collected by Malorie Blackman, Corgi Books, 2007

TRAFFICK SPOTTING

- ◢ Was someone being trafficked when I last caught a flight?
- ◢ Has a trafficked person made my clothes or chocolate?
- ◢ Are trafficked people working on a farm near me?
- ◢ Was the homeless child who asked me for money last week trafficked?

Become part of the fight to stop people being trafficked simply by seeing signs of trafficking going on when you're in your local high street, catching a flight or in a restaurant.

If you see it, report it.

LOOK FOR THESE SIGNS

ON A FARM OR IN A FACTORY...

▲ Farm or factory workers using poor or **NON-EXISTENT SAFETY EQUIPMENT**

▲ WORKERS **WITHOUT SUITABLE CLOTHING** for the work they are doing

▲ Workers living in **OVERCROWDED** private rented accommodation. They don't know the address of where they live or work

▲ Minibuses picking up non-nationals at **UNUSUAL HOURS**, day and night

▲ Bins at the accommodation full of fast-food packaging

▲ Workers who seem **FEARFUL** and poorly integrated into the wider community

▲ Workers who have no days off or holiday time

▲ An employer or someone else holding their **PASSPORT** and legal documents.

DOMESTIC LABOUR...

▲ An adult or child who lives with a family nearby, possibly as a **DOMESTIC SERVANT** or **NANNY**

▲ Domestic workers who are rarely allowed out of the house, unless their employer or guardian is with them

▲ Domestic workers who are subject to **ABUSE**, insults, threats or violence

▲ No private space or a place to sleep, sleeping on the floor or sofa

▲ Evidence of a **POOR DIET** or family's leftover food to eat

▲ If the worker is a child, poor attendance at school, no access to education and no time to play

▲ A lack of much **INTERACTION** with the family.

IF YOU ARE TRAVELLING...

▲ A child who is **TRAVELLING ALONE**

▲ A child who does not seem to have many possessions but who has a **MOBILE PHONE**

▲ A child who is not travelling to meet his or her parent or guardian

▲ A child who is **SUSPICIOUS OF ADULTS**

▲ A child who is very **AFRAID OF BEING DEPORTED**

▲ A child who shows signs of **INAPPROPRIATE OR SEXUALIZED BEHAVIOUR** towards men.

IN A SAUNA OR MASSAGE PARLOUR...

▲ A woman who appears to be **UNHAPPY AND UNWILLING TO PERFORM SEXUAL ACTS**

▲ A woman who is **FRIGHTENED** or in physical **PAIN**

▲ A woman who sees a large number of clients each day/night

▲ A woman who is able to keep little, or none, of the money that she receives from clients

▲ 'Special' services offered including unprotected sex, often at a **LOW PRICE**

▲ A woman who doesn't smile and is **RELUCTANT** to cooperate

▲ Food is paid for by another person

▲ A woman who has little or no time off

▲ A woman who may only know how to say sex-related words in English.

ON YOUR HIGH STREET...

◢ A young, elderly or disabled foreign national who **BEGS IN PUBLIC PLACES OR ON PUBLIC TRANSPORT**

◢ A person showing obvious signs of being **ABUSED**, such as **BRUISES, CUTS OR MUTILATION**

◢ A person who seems fearful of adults (especially law enforcers) or whose behaviour is jumpy

◢ One adult is the guardian of a large group of children

◢ A large group of adult or child beggars are **MOVED** daily to different locations but return to the same location every night

◢ On public transport they **MOVE AS A GROUP**, such as walking up and down the length or a train or bus.

YOU OR SOMEONE YOU KNOW...

◢ A **TEENAGE GIRL** who has met an older male who becomes her boyfriend. Initially he flatters her, buys her gifts such as a mobile phone, and introduces her to alcohol or drugs. He makes her feel incredibly special

◢ The man **CONTROLS** her more and more. He claims she owes him for drugs and forces her to do sexual favours as a means of payment

◢ SHE **IS TAKEN** from her family home and returned after varying lengths of time; her relationship with her family or guardians gradually becomes severed

◢ Pictures or films of her engaging in sex activities are used to make her feel **GUILTY**, fearful her family will find out. Her 'boyfriend' uses this to control her, making her sleep with his friends

◢ He takes her to different flats (even in different towns or cities), getting her to sleep with different men

◢ She may not know he is taking **PAYMENT** from these men either in money or illegal drugs.

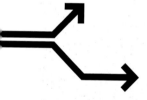

FORM AN ACT GROUP

Form Active Communities against Trafficking (ACT) groups as a means to allow people of all ages, ethnicities and genders in a local community to:

◢ Understand sex trafficking
◢ Understand how it affects our local community
◢ Respond in a proactive way that will lead to a reduction of sex trafficking.

There are different ways for ACT groups to engage with sex trafficking in your area and there are two STOP THE TRAFFIK packs designed to cater for this:

AWARENESS AND ACTION PACK
The pack, primarily aimed at under eighteens and others uncomfortable making direct contact with the sex industry, provides educational tools and ideas for action.

COMMUNITY INFORMATION PACK
The focus of this pack is to train and equip groups (over 18s only) so they can: collect objective information about their local sex industry and highlight areas of concern, build relationships with professional agencies and provide them with information so they can proactively respond to sex trafficking.

If you are interested in forming an ACT group, see the START chapter and visit www.stopthetraffik.org.

REPORT ANYTHING SUSPICIOUS TO:

Stop (Trafficking UK):
Telephone 0844 800 33 14

Crimestoppers:
Telephone 0800 555 111

NSPCC Child Trafficking
Advice and Information Line:
0800 107 7057

IN AN EMERGENCY, PLEASE DIAL 999

THINK

Who do you think is vulnerable to being trafficked? And how do you think those vulnerabilities are exploited to create a worldwide trade in people?

SONIA'S STORY

'I am not a victim.'

Sonia has curly brown hair and olive skin. She is self-possessed and looks you defiantly in the eye when she talks about her life. When she was just a child, Sonia began working as a prostitute in her native Mexico. Eventually she was evicted from home at the age of fourteen. Although Sonia tried to get other jobs, she couldn't, and she always ended up returning to prostitution.

When she was seventeen, a taxi driver invited Sonia to go to Europe. With her striking Latin looks, he said, she could probably work as a model and make a fortune. He would take care of all the arrangements. Sonia was tempted by the money, but frightened, too. After more persuasion she accepted his offer. It took the man a month to arrange everything for her. Three other girls went with them.

When they arrived in Europe, still excited, still hopeful, another taxi driver took their passports. He told them to trust him since the city was very dangerous. Little did Sonia know that the real danger was him.

Sonia and her three friends were forced to work every day from 6 p.m. to 6 a.m. as prostitutes, and were told that they would not get their passports back before the house manager was paid back for the travel arrangements. Sonia says she expected prostitution, but had never imagined she would be a prisoner, living in fear, threatened day and night.

UNITED NATIONS OFFICE ON DRUGS AND CRIME (UNODC)

It is a mistake to imagine that all trafficking victims are the same: the truth is a more complex. Trafficked people come from all kinds of backgrounds, and have widely differing beliefs and personalities. Many of those who are trafficked into the sex trade are, like Sonia, already a part of it. Yet it would be wrong to conclude that they were 'asking for trouble', and deserved what happened to them.

> **'I despise nobody... because if our circumstances were the same, we should surely all become the same, and our circumstances lie beyond our control.'**
>
> **GEORG BÜCHNER (1813–37)**

It's important we avoid judging women like Sonia. Until we really know the circumstances, the poverty and hardship, that have led someone to make the 'choice' – if it can be called that – to enter into prostitution, we can't begin to understand. And yet however hard that choice may be, there is still a significant difference between 'voluntary' prostitution, where a woman has, at least in theory, an element of control, and the violent terror of forced prostitution when a woman has no control, no money, no safety, hope or choice. It is the latter that we are concerned with in this book. Nobody deserves to be trafficked.

The romantic comedy *Pretty Woman*, the story of a prostitute who marries a rich businessman, is considered to be the most popular film in the Ukraine. Often girls trafficked to the US have been tricked or misled and hope for the same fairytale ending. But that fairytale becomes a nightmare: there is rarely a happy ending.

NASREEN'S STORY

Nasreen was one of the lucky few who lived to tell her tale. She was a young, lively Tajik girl who worked in Moscow. Her boss asked her to become his mistress, promising money, housing, a car and a better life. Nasreen agreed to to this arrangement: it was the best job offer she'd ever had.

One day, a houseguest offered Nasreen the opportunity to work in Turkey. Nasreen's boss pressured her to accept the offer. Nasreen was tricked, and trafficked to Israel into forced prostitution. Instead of the one man she'd agreed to live with, Nasreen was subjected to rape by dozens of strangers.

With the help of a sympathetic journalist, Nasreen was able to escape and return home. But the trauma of her story is still being experienced by thousands of others.

US STATE DEPARTMENT *ANNUAL TRAFFICKING IN PERSONS REPORT*

Did Nasreen have it coming? Like Sonia, Nasreen was offering herself for money; she was fully prepared to be someone's mistress. This is what people are driven to do because of severe poverty. But the reality was far more brutal than what she had signed up for.

Woman handing over her passport.

The police have sometimes been surprised at the kind of victims they have found. There was an assumption that trafficking victims would be just that; helpless victims, innocents forced into the harsh realities of the world, stay-at-homes, forced out rather than migrating willingly. They expected that victims would be ready to talk, to testify. But the victims are not always forthcoming. A police interview can be worrying for anyone, but for a trafficking victim to talk to anyone about their experience is traumatic. Many have experienced suffering we can only begin to imagine. Violently beaten, raped repeatedly, often for hours of every day. This is not an easy thing to talk about. And there is a sense in which they may feel implicated if they have co-operated with their traffickers at the start.

Many women, such as Sonia and Nasreen, are worldly wise, and do not fit a distressed maiden stereotype. Their hardships have forced them into an early knowledge of the injustices of the world. Their childhoods have been swallowed up by brutality. Their experiences have toughened them.

This worldliness, so surprising to the CO14 officers, has been forced upon these women, often as a result of poverty. This can range from relative poverty – a struggle to make ends meet – to severe destitution. Anyone within this spectrum is susceptible to trafficking, as they are often looking for a better life, better opportunities and more money.

'You never really understand a person until you consider things from his point of view – until you climb into his skin and walk around in it.'

ATTICUS FINCH, TO KILL A MOCKINGBIRD, *HARPER LEE ARROW BOOKS, 2006, © HARPER LEE, 1960*

Not all victims of trafficking set out on their journey unwillingly. There are many who agree to being transported to another country to work, thinking they are being taken to a better life. Many women go overseas expecting to work as a waitress, au pair or maid, only to discover on arrival that they have been sold into forced prostitution. Whether it is women trafficked into sex slavery, or boys trafficked into cocoa farms, they spend their journey in hope. It is only at their destination that the horrifying reality becomes clear.

POVERTY

Poverty drives people to extremes. But even here the trafficked person is portrayed as a 'faint-hearted individual succumbing to temptation'. Many of them may, in fact, start out a lot more strong-willed than that. And then, all too often, as with Maria, who was interviewed by the UNODC, their spirits are crushed.

MARIA'S STORY

'I started living on the streets when I was eleven years old – my father threw my brother and me out of the house. He never worried about us – he was always taking alcohol combined with drugs. On the streets, I met prostitution and crime. One always dreams about being somebody, and that having material things makes you somebody. I never imagined that, wanting to improve my living conditions, I was going to end up losing my dignity.'

MARIA FERNANDA, INTERVIEWED BY THE UNODC COUNTRY OFFICE IN COLOMBIA, PUBLISHED IN UN, 2008.

Desperate situations lead to desperate solutions. But in many cases, trafficking feeds off not extreme poverty, but disparity of wealth. In other words, someone relatively poor knows there are richer countries out there, where they could earn more money, and this kindles a desire to migrate. This, in turn, leaves them vulnerable to the wiles of traffickers offering them an easy route into that 'dream country' – only to find a horrifying life of slavery waiting for them.

> Poverty is a great force that drives an individual to think the unthinkable and do the undoable. The desperate need for money and the lack of alternate means and ways to generate income creates an environment where a faint-hearted individual can easily succumb to the temptation of wealth that a sex industry has to offer.

NEWSLETTER MAILTI NEPAL – IS POVERTY THE ONLY REASON?
VOL.1, NO.4, MAY–JUNE 1999

Cultural factors also offer traffickers a way in. In many countries, especially in South Asia, girls being bought and sold is widespread. Parents are often expected to pay a dowry to their daughter's future husband. By putting a price on her, this tradition sets the girl up as saleable goods in her own eyes, and everybody else's.

Girls are often seen as being 'on loan' to their own families until they are married, when they 'belong' to their husband and his family. In either situation they are expected to work for their family. The effect of these practices on a woman's self-esteem – and on the path she takes in life – is enormous.

And a trafficker will exploit these traditions. He may offer to marry a girl – especially if her parents are poor and stand to benefit from her marriage. Traffickers will often remove the need for parents to pay a dowry – money they are desperately keen to save. But once married, the trafficker has control over the girl, to do with as he pleases.

POVERTY AND TRAFFICKING

The countries mentioned below are major 'origin' countries: many people who are trafficked come from these countries.

◢ In Moldova one-third of all children live in poverty.

◢ In Moldova, 68% of the unemployed people are women.

Moldova Gender Profile: World Bank

◢ In the last decade approximately 60% of the unemployed people in Romania were women; 68% in Russia.

– UNESCO: The Feminisation of Poverty and Women's Human Rights

◢ In Albania nearly 25% of the population lived below the poverty line (2002).

World Development Report: Equality and Development Background Papers

◢ An estimated 42% of the population lives below the poverty line in Nepal.

Asian development bank, Country Profile Nepal (www.adb.org/gender/final_nepal.pdf)

◢ The United Nations has stated that in the Ukraine, poverty is THE cause of human trafficking.

A family from Moldova. Due to poverty, the father works away for several months at a time, leaving his sixteen-year-old daughter to look after her sister and brothers. This exposes them to traffickers.

Poverty, domestic violence and a lack of education fed directly into Zofia's story of trafficking and abuse. There is no doubt that it was the lure of money that drove Zofia's own sister to sell her to a trafficker.

ZOFIA'S STORY

'My name is Zofia and I am twenty-four years old. I have been raped, beaten, sold, cut with knives and threatened. I have scars and I am depressed.

I come from a very poor family and grew up in the countryside of an Eastern European country. I did not regularly attend school and did not have a good formal education. When I lived at home my father used to drink a lot. He would beat me and my family. When I was thirteen my sister sold me, to a man I did not know. He took me to Italy by boat, which was very dangerous. I did not know where I was going. Once we arrived in Italy I was sold again, to a different man. He took me to a house and raped me. I was a virgin until then.

It was then that I realized what was happening to me. I started crying and the man started to beat me, hard. But neighbours overheard me screaming and called the police, who took me away and left me in a nunnery for protection. I was returned home to my family after two years. But just four days later I was sold again, this time by my father.

He sold me to a different man, but now I knew what was happening to me. Again we went by boat to Italy, where I was kept prisoner for seven months. They controlled my eating and made me drink vinegar. Finally I was smuggled into the UK in a lorry. I was in London for five years. I worked every day, seeing sixty-five to seventy customers a day. I could earn up to £1,000 per day, but I had to pay £400 every day in 'rent' and £60 for a maid, as well as twenty per cent of everything else I earned.

The men who came to me were of all different nationalities. I did not ask any of them for help. I was too frightened. My traffickers threatened to kill me, and they threatened to take my sister too and do the same to her. I was beaten often, very badly. I have scars from it now, especially from my broken arm. I have been raped many times.

I finally escaped with the other women in my house. We ran away with the owner's boyfriend and went to the police.

Although I am now free I am depressed. I will never forget what they did to me.'

UK HUMAN TRAFFICKING CENTRE
(www.ukhtc.org)

BREAKING THE CYCLE OF POVERTY

Throughout the world, and especially in developing countries, women are at a disadvantage. All the figures show that overall women are less well-educated, have fewer job opportunities, and less control over their own bodies.

Girls find it harder to break the cycle of poverty. They are less equipped with skills to improve their situations.

Poverty is not just about money: it is about quality of life. Many women are not only poor, but denied the chance of escaping from poverty. They are denied education and work. Yet globally, there continues to be a massive demand for cheap female labour.

Maybe you thought we were living in an enlightened age and that women are equal now. Well, think again.

Millions of women are still being oppressed. And for them, the only way to change their lives is to migrate – which exposes them to the risk of trafficking.

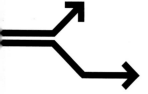

A woman trafficked into sexual exploitation is rescued by police in India through the work of SACMEP.

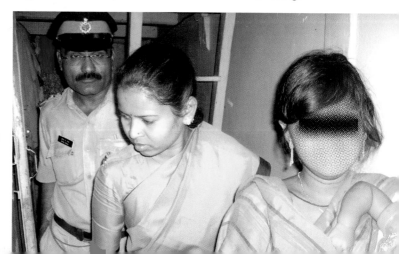

IMMIGRATION

It is all too easy to shrug off the presence of these people as an immigration problem. Of course, that is not the case at all – much of the time trafficking victims have no idea where they are being taken, where they will end up. They need our help, not our contempt.

> **'Traffickers fish in the stream of migration.'**
>
> **UN RAPPORTEUR,** *ASIAN DEVELOPMENT BANK,*
> *COUNTRY PROFILE: NEPAL*

All that migrants want is to earn enough money to survive, enough money to feed their family. These are people like you and me. They are prepared to work hard, and honestly, to care for the ones they love. Yet they are being exploited.

… If it were you, what would you do?…

Imagine the daily grind of poverty, unemployment, domestic violence, the horrors of war and natural disasters. Invariably this is what trafficked people – most of them women – have experienced.

Many of them have been denied access to education, have limited job opportunities, and in some cases have had little opportunity to change what happens in their own countries.

> **No job, no rights, no voice.**
> **No safety, hope or choice.**

Many of those being trafficked come from areas of high emigration such as Moldova, Albania, Romania and Bulgaria.

Many of these women choose to migrate to a wealthier country, aiming for a better standard of living and to earn money to send home to their families.

If your country's economy was falling apart, if jobs were scarce, and you had a hungry family needing food, perhaps medicine… If it were you, what would you do?

Entering departures at the airport in Tirana, Albania.

'Women and girls may themselves take the initiative to migrate in the hope of earning a decent income, escaping a miserable life, or supporting a family back home. In such cases, they are sometimes aware that they are going to work in commercial sex, considering this to be an acceptable short-term remedy to a desperate need to earn a living. They very rarely, however, are aware of the nature of the demands that will be made upon them, the conditions in which they are likely to be held, or the possible long-term repercussions of the activity.'

INTERNATIONAL LABOR ORGANIZATION (ILO)

Not all trafficking is through migration across international borders – many people are being trafficked without leaving the country.

Migration is absolutely necessary in a globalized world – and migration always involves more hidden dangers for women than for men.

Women and girls are more vulnerable to discrimination, sexual abuse and exploitation. Of course, not all migrants are trafficked persons, but while migrating, women especially are vastly more vulnerable to traffickers and exploitation networks (www.iom.int/jahia/webdav/site/myjahiasite/shared/shared/mainsite/media/sp/Discours_Haifa_sep05_Eng.pdf).

Let's replace this climate of fear with SAFETY, HOPE and CHOICE.

MARINA'S STORY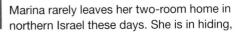

Marina rarely leaves her two-room home in northern Israel these days. She is in hiding, wanted by the Israeli authorities for being an undocumented immigrant whose papers had been taken from her by her traffickers, and by the criminal gangs who brought her here to sell her into prostitution.

... If it were you, what would you do?...

Marina was lured to Israel by human traffickers. Like Marina, some trafficked women are brought into the country legally, while others are smuggled by Bedouins across the border from Egypt.

During the height of the phenomenon, from the beginning of the 1990s to the early years of 2000, an estimated 3,000 women a year were brought to Israel on the false promise of jobs and a better way of life.

'When I was in the Ukraine, I had a difficult life,' said Marina, who came to Israel in 1999 at the age of thirty-three after answering a newspaper advertisement offering the opportunity to study abroad.

'I was taken to an apartment in Ashkelon, and other women there told me I was now in prostitution. I became hysterical, but a guy starting hitting me and then others there raped me.

'I was then taken to a place where they sold me – just sold me!' she said, recalling how she was locked in a windowless basement for a month, drank water from a toilet and was deprived of food.

That part of her ordeal ended only when she managed to escape, but the physical and mental scars remain (*http://uruknet.info/?p=m38585&s1=h1*).

Rich countries like the UK are closing their borders to unskilled workers. People who are desperate to leave their countries in their current state – women ground down by poverty with no hope of a better life at home – have no chance of getting in legally. This means they find alternative ways of escape. And this is where the trafficking networks come in, exploiting need.

In countries such as India, Pakistan, Bangladesh and the Philippines, governments attempt to protect women from abuse abroad by trying to control female migration. But this also forces desperate women underground.

Safer, more open migration networks would allow desperate people more freedom – and make the lives of traffickers much harder. These measures have to be combined with efforts of reform in their home countries – migration is not the only answer.

This is not about increasing levels of migration. If we welcome those migrants who do make it to our country, we offer them safety, hope and choice. They are less vulnerable to traffickers. And that can only be a good thing.

POTENTIAL SOLUTIONS

◢ **Enable people to migrate more safely**

◢ **Regulate employment and travel agencies**

◢ **Make sure labour standards are enforced**

◢ **Train/educate potential migrants, e.g. Safe Migration scheme set up by Street Friends (**www.streetfriends.org/CONTENT/in_action/young_ migrants.html**).**

In Leeds there are several projects aimed at promoting safe migration. These are ground-breaking ideas which enrich the community and also increase safety for vulnerable people. Could your town do the same?

◢ Asylum seekers befriending scheme.

This is for people claiming asylum but could be extended to migrants (both documented and undocumented).

There are three principal activities:

1. TEACHING ENGLISH

2. PROVIDING EMERGENCY BED SPACE
◢ Volunteers provide emergency shelter for a night or two in their homes

◢ They provide an evening meal and breakfast and a bed/sofa.

◢ In some cases volunteers have given bed space to rescued and escaped trafficked women – essential refuge for people who have experienced intense trauma.

3. BEFRIENDING
◢ The scheme has had massive success helping people connect with local communities

◢ Volunteers meet an asylum seeker on a regular basis

◢ Volunteers provide information on services, help numbers, counsellors, socializing

◢ The biggest success has been a clear improvement in the mental health and happiness levels of asylum seekers

◢ Leeds has launched a 'Leeds, City of welcome' campaign, designed specifically to welcome migrants.

Rickshaws in Mumbai.

CULTURE

ATTITUDES TO WOMEN

A team from South Asia Centre for Missing and Exploited Persons (SACMEP) led an investigation in the city of Mumbai in India, one of the world's mega cities with a population of at least nineteen million. Pretending to be people who wanted to buy a girl, SACMEP spoke to rickshaw drivers, who linked them to a woman called Bharti. Bharti, about thirty-five and married with one son, was a full-time human trafficker.

BHARTI'S STORY

She was an ordinary woman, of medium height, wearing a lot of gold and obviously well dressed, with a good mobile phone and lots of cash on her, living in a middle-class area of Malad, a suburb of Mumbai. She was anything but ordinary, though. Originally from West Bengal in the east of India, she had previously been a prostitute. Whether she had been trafficked or not is unknown, but it is possible. She had now become a trafficker, visiting villages around the area she came from, with her husband, promising the girls a good job in the city of Mumbai. When they agreed to go with her, she took them and sold them into prostitution. The SACMEP team conducted a difficult raid with the police, and rescued a child she had trafficked into prostitution. Bharti is now in jail, waiting for the trial.

Bharti looked pretty harmless. But she was a trafficker. Perhaps you thought all traffickers would somehow look different, exuding evil. Yet very often they look just like you or me. And that's how they trap people.

Nepalese children are rescued by the EBT and returned to their families.

YOUR RESPONSE

How do you view women? How do you view yourself? Your knee-jerk reaction may be that you believe in equal rights for women. That you believe in justice for all. You're a fair-minded kind of person.

But simmering beneath the surface, are there any assumptions bubbling away that may not help women to be perceived as truly equal?

In the developing world, this issue is not just simmering – it has reached boiling point. In many places, boys are often viewed as superior. Infanticide rates show a strong preference for boys, and girls are much more likely to be aborted once their gender is known.

These are attitudes that make women more susceptible to low self-esteem and reduced opportunities. And from there to being trafficked is just a step. Traffickers single out the 'victims' and pounce.

Jorge was interviewed by UNODC Country Office in Columbia, published in *Human Trafficking: An Overview* in 2008. His attitude to the women he preys on shows he views them virtually as objects. He focuses on their physical attributes and sizes them up.

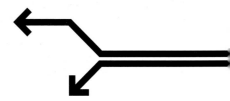

> 'First I was a sex worker, and I know working in prostitution is hard, more for a man, but in any case it was a business that didn't fill my money expectations... so I got involved with the Yakuza [Japanese organized crime group]. To avoid losing money... you must learn how to identify the victims.'
>
> 'For example, looking at the moles in their ears, you know if they're good for the money or not, and from their lips you know if they're good in bed or not. You go to a disco or a restaurant, looking for the girls who fill the profile: medium height, white skin, slim... you convince them, and send them as soon as possible. It's a high-profit business.'

But is what Jorge says much different from the way people in a nightclub check each other out? Think about it. Are your attitudes that different from this trafficker?

> '...Ekta said that the men liked them to be young and sometimes fear pleased them too. Neela was just sixteen and she was very afraid'.

SUSAN LEWIS,
INTIMATE STRANGERS, 2003

> 'We learned responses. Like if they wanted us to be sultry or sexy or scared. Most of them wanted you scared. When I got older I'd teach kids how to float away so things didn't hurt'.

GIRL TRAFFICKED INTO SEX SLAVERY,
NEW YORK TIMES, 25 JANUARY 2005

Imagine, then, the draw of a culture where women are seen to be empowered, where they are given education and jobs. Imagine what such a place must seem like to these girls – paradise compared with home.

For many women they will do what they can to get there.

PORNOGRAPHY

You might think of it as harmless fun. Or maybe you disapprove of the messages it sends out. But whatever your view on porn, did it ever occur to you that people are being forced into it?

The fact is that trafficked girls and women are often forced to participate in the growing Internet pornography industry.

Experts have found links between the growing human trafficking industry and the growing pornography industry. This is an industry in which the U.S. plays a huge role: 89 per cent of pornographic websites belong to the United States (*www.toptenreviews.com*).

Pornography is just one manifestation of the way the West perceives women. Women are socialized from birth to be submissive to men – and this puts them at huge risk of trafficking.

Do we ever see women as sex objects, devaluing or stereotyping their sexuality? Are strip-clubs and brothels promoting women as vacuous commodities? Too often, women's bodies are being rated out of ten – their intellect and abilities forgotten.

GIRLS IN DEVELOPING COUNTRIES

◢ In rural Mexico, 40% of girls spend twenty hours a week on household chores, in addition to school.

◢ One in seven girls in developing countries are married by fifteen.

◢ By twenty, 50% are married.

◢ In developing countries fourteen million girls between fifteen and nineteen give birth every year – and are five times more likely to die from complications.

◢ In Kenya, 46% of women experienced sexual abuse as a child.

Girls Count (www.cgdev.org/content/publications/detail/15154)

'I felt like a piece of flesh being inspected.'

SEE NOI'S STORY, CHAPTER 2: LOOK

ROSHNI'S STORY

A petite young girl with a shy but endearing smile, Roshni, twenty, is extremely hard-working and has mastered the skill of Aari work, which is a type of embroidery using colourful beads, threads and sequins.

Just a few years ago, her life was completely different. On being promised employment, Roshni agreed to come to Mumbai in India from her home town in Andhra Pradesh – but was horrified to find herself in a brothel. It was then that she realized that her relative, whom she trusted, had in fact deceived her and sold her into the flesh trade. Roshni was still an under-age girl.

When the police conducted a raid at the brothel, Roshni was rescued and sent to a home which provided care for girls until the age of eighteen. She was tested HIV-positive.

On turning eighteen, Roshni was sent to Purnata Bhavan, (a residential care project of Oasis India, www.oasisindia.org), where she participated in the literacy programmes offered and learnt to read and write. She also became so skilled at Aari work that she is now able to teach others. Roshni would soon be doing an advanced course in Aari work before she could start working.

OASIS INDIA

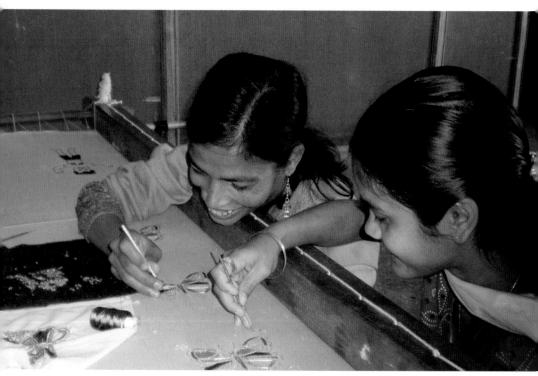

Two women doing aari work at Oasis India's project in Purata Bhavan.

FORCED LABOUR

For girls like Roshni, so brutally used as a child sex slave, education is the route to another life.

Education opens up vistas of possibility. Yet it is being denied to thousands of women across the globe.

Often if a family can afford to send only one child to school, it will be the boy who goes. Girls are much more likely to be expected to help at home or with domestic service.

EDUCATION OF ASSISTED VICTIMS

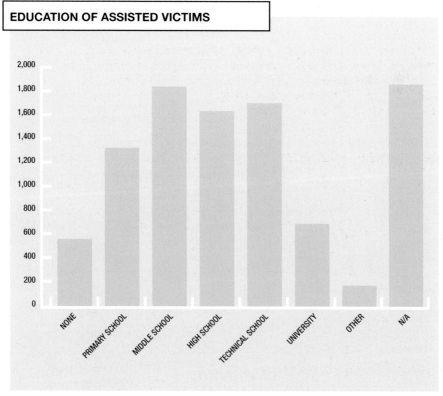

IOM Counter Trafficking Database

As this chart shows, people being trafficked who are completely without education are relatively rare. Poverty, even for those who have some education, will always drive people across borders, and into the hands of traffickers. For Marta, even having an education did not prevent her from being trafficked.

Education can help people escape trafficking. But it is powerless in the face of poverty.

MARTA'S STORY

Marta is a bright, engaging girl from Central America, with a Bachelor's Degree in Business Administration. She went to the US on a tourist visa to work and send money back home to her family. The poverty in her country did not allow her to make enough money to support her family, so she was willing to work as a maid, even with her education.

Marta was taken to a beautiful home in one of the most affluent areas in southwest Florida and given a job as a housekeeper. Little did she know that she had actually been sold in her home country to become a domestic slave.

The travel agency that she had gone through to come to the US was actually a trafficking agency.

Once in place with the family, Marta was enslaved and not allowed to leave. She asked permission to use the bathroom but had to go outside to the pool bathroom. She slept on the pebbles in the pool area and was attacked by mosquitoes that left scars all over her body.

The traffickers allowed her to eat once a week, so she was forced to wrap small portions of food in plastic to be retrieved later from the garbage can.

Marta was allowed to attend church once a week, provided she obtained the name and address of each of the church members. One week, her trafficker told her he would be a few minutes late and she took the opportunity to speak with the pastor and tell him her situation. They planned her escape for the next Sunday.

When arriving at the church the following Sunday, Marta was whisked away out of the back of the church to safety. When the trafficker arrived to pick her up and she was not there, they went looking for her at each of the addresses and finally found her. They made such a commotion that the police were called and the advocate realized that this was a case of trafficking. So Marta managed to escape.

Today Marta is happily married and owns her own business in the US.

But she still afraid to go out, as her traffickers eluded prosecution and are still on the loose (*http://stophumantrafficking.org/News.htm*).

Amongst trafficked women, Marta's education is relatively unusual.

In some developing countries and countries plagued by trafficking, illiteracy amongst girls remains more common than amongst boys.

Imagine being unable to read. Unable to explore your own identity through reading the words of others, or writing down your own thoughts. How would that affect how you see yourself?

EDUCATION AND TRAFFICKING

◢ In Nepal, 'districts that have the highest rates of female illiteracy, such as Nuwakot and Sindhupalchowk, with illiteracy 90% and 92% respectively, are also among the worst districts for girl trafficking.'

World Education – Nepal

◢ In 2001, 21.7% of the adult population were literate in Nepal.

Asian development bank,
Country Profile Nepal (www.adb.org/gender/final_nepal.pdf)

◢ In sub-Saharan Africa, 68% of young girls describe themselves as illiterate.

New York Times, 25 Jan 2005

◢ Education 'offers the child an improved opportunity to be less dependent on men in later like. It increases her prospect of obtaining work outside the home.'

UN Factsheet 23

◢ Just under 50% of women in Uganda and 50% of women in Tanzania were abused by a male teacher.

Girls Count (www.cgdev.org/content/publications/detail/15154)

Illiteracy is isolating. If a girl is illiterate, it contributes to her lack of self-esteem, and her limited options. And if she migrates, she can be taken anywhere by a trafficker and not even read the place names. She is lost.

Yet, as we saw with Marta, not even an education can get in the way of a determined trafficker. In Albania, illiteracy is not a problem – but trafficking is.

Disparity of wealth is the primary factor in trafficking, with illiteracy simply increasing a girl's chances of being vulnerable.

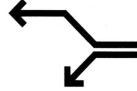

Sign to airport terminal in Tirana, Albania.

LINDITA'S STORY

In the case of Lindita, an Albanian girl with an intense gaze, she had an education. But she fell in love, and just happened to trust the wrong man. It could happen to anybody.

'When I was a senior in high school here in Tirana, I met a boy who did not go to my school. He was kind, attractive, and treated me well. After a time, we fell in love with each other – or so I thought at the time. He was my "first love", and I hadn't had much experience with boys romantically prior to that.

After dating for a time, he convinced me to go to Belgium with him. He said that he could get a good job there and told me about what a wonderful place it was: how clean, how beautiful, and how many opportunities there would be there for us. He proposed to me, and our plan was to leave Albania illegally (since we would not qualify for visas) and get married once he found work there. **I was in love, and I believed him.'**

… If it were you, what would you do?…

'Once we got to Belgium, however, he totally changed. He became abusive of me and violated me many times. He threatened my life and the lives of my family members. **I did not speak the language there and was totally dependent on him**; I had nowhere else to go and was afraid. He trafficked me for six months. I don't want to talk anymore about that time. **It was the worst period in my life**. It is now in my past, and I have closed that door behind me.

I was able to find a shelter there with people to help me return to Albania. I wanted to return to my family here, **but my father would not accept me** and was abusive of me and my mother.

My mother decided to leave my father to help me, even though this is something unheard of in Albania for a woman to leave her husband. Women here can't really find work to support themselves and have to rely on their fathers or husbands for their livelihood. My mother gave up everything for me, and for this I am grateful.

After living in the shelter for as long as we were allowed, **my mother and I are now living together and trying to support ourselves**' (www.humantrafficking. com/humantrafficking/features_ht3/Testimonies/testimonies_mainframe.htm).

Lindita's story is fascinating. Her father blames her for being trafficked. To him she has been tainted by the abuses she has suffered. Her mother leaving her father was virtually unheard of. It is rare for women to support themselves.

All these factors keep women subservient. And that gives traffickers an easy way in to exploit them.

A trafficking survivor BMS has been involved in supporting through their work in Albanian prisons.

ATTITUDES TO BOYS

How we think about trafficking is clearly related to women and girls. But thousands of boys are also being trafficked. Despite frequent cultural advantages over girls, the root causes of trafficking such as poverty still make boys vulnerable to trafficking.

SHADIR'S STORY

Shadir, a sparky, intelligent Indian boy of fifteen, was offered a job that, he was told, would include good clothes and an education. Feeling excited, he accepted. But instead of being given a job, Shadir was sold to a slave trader, who took him to a remote village in India to produce hand-woven carpets.

Shadir was frequently beaten. He worked twelve to fourteen hours a day and he was poorly fed. Life became unbearable. One day, Shadir was rescued from his torment by an non-governmental organization (NGO) working to combat slavery.

He was so traumatized by his experiences that it took several days for Shadir to realize he was no longer enslaved. He returned to his village, was reunited with his mother, and resumed his schooling. Now Shadir warns fellow village children about the risks of becoming a child slave.

US DEPARTMENT OF STATE (www.state.gov/g/tip/c16482.htm)

Boys like Shadir are being trafficked into forced labour. But they're also being trafficked into the sex industry.

So when you think about sex trafficking, don't just think about girls and women. Spare a thought for the boys affected as well.

Our attitudes in the West also feed into this issue. True, boys are often given more opportunities than girls. But think a little harder. You've probably heard stories and even jokes about young boys at boarding school being abused by the older boys.

But if we joke about this, does that mean we're devaluing the sexuality of boys? They have a right to childhood innocence just as much as girls.

And for those boys being abused by traffickers around the globe, this is no joke.

1. Globally, more women than men are uneducated, illiterate or unemployed. Can you prove this is not so? Do a search on the Internet for statistics and background for evidence to the contrary.

2. Watch yourself during the course of a normal day. Ask yourself : do I view women differently to men? Do I value their opinions less than those of men? Do I put women down?

3. Think about the women closest to you when you were growing up. What can you remember about the way they related to men and other women? What has changed? What hasn't?

MORE TO THINK ABOUT

This defiance is summed up in Harriet Beecher Stowe's ground-breaking anti-slavery novel of 1852, *Uncle Tom's Cabin*:

'... Ain't I yer master? Didn't I pay down twelve hundred dollars, cash, for all there is inside yer old cussed black shell? An't yer mine, now, body and soul?' he said, giving Tom a violent kick with his heavy boot; 'tell me!'

In the very depth of physical suffering, bowed by brutal oppression, this question shot a gleam of joy and triumph through Tom's soul. He suddenly stretched himself up, and, looking earnestly to heaven, while the tears and blood that flowed down his face mingled, he exclaimed, 'No! no! no! my soul ain't yours, Mas'r! You haven't bought it, – ye can't buy it! It's been bought and paid for, by one that is able to keep it; – no matter, no matter, you can't harm me!'

Copy of anti-slavery novel Uncle Tom's Cabin.

CHAPTER 5

A chocolate bar: just a harmless treat?
But who picked those cocoa beans?
Is there a darker side to your chocolate?
Money to spend, choices to make –
don't buy into the global trade of people.

We rarely see the link between something that we buy and the person who helped pick its ingredients. But we *are* linked, in a very important way: by a supply chain that starts at producers, and via industry, reaches us, the consumers. These supply chains are often opaque; we are unable to see what goes on. This means cruel, exploitative practices can creep in at any level.

The good news is that we can buy a guilt-free chocolate bar. We can buy dozens. We can buy fairtrade. It's that simple. Buying fairtrade chocolate – or tea, coffee, bananas or cotton – is the best way of knowing that what you're getting is free from human trafficking. And the more we buy fairtrade, the more we send out the message that anything produced by trafficking is unacceptable.

Put your money where your mouth is.

Cocoa flow

Farmers

Individual buyers

Traders

Buying centres

Exporters

Chocolate manufacturers

Shops

You

'If you eat chocolate that isn't traffick free, then you've got blood on your teeth.'

RHYS IFANS

A TRAFFICKED CHILD, AGE TEN When I was ten, I left home to try and earn some money to help my family. When I got to Sikasso, I didn't know anyone. A locater found me at the bus station and asked me if I was looking for work. He told me that the work in Mali is not worth my trouble; that I should go to Korhogo, and when I get there, I could make lots of money. I told him that I could not say that this was true, because I have never been to Korhogo and that I was too small to go. But I could not get away from him and he talked and talked and convinced... me. He put me in his car and we went to Ivory Coast and sold me to a planter for 20,000 CFA ($40).

ILRF

It is hard to equate the pleasure of chocolate with the pain too often involved in its production. Yet, thousands of children – no one knows exactly how many – have been trafficked into the Ivory Coast to pick the cocoa that makes our chocolate.

Some work on family farms. But even here, abuses can occur.

Boys working on a cocoa plantation on the Ivory Coast.

IVORY COAST FACTS

▲ The Ivory Coast (also known as Côte d'Ivoire, in West Africa) is the biggest producer of cocoa in the world, with around 40% of the world supply coming from that country.

▲ There are more than 600,000 cocoa farms in the Ivory Coast, most of them small family farms.

▲ Cocoa is the main economic resource of the country, representing on average 35% of the total value of Ivorian exports, worth around US$1.4billion per year.

▲ Ivory Coast has experienced prolonged instability since a military coup in 1999. After an army-led rebellion in September 2002, a peace agreement in 2003 established a government in which representatives of the rebel group Forces Nouvelles (FN) held ministerial positions.

▲ A new peace deal was signed on 4 March 2007, when FN leader Guillaume Sao became prime minister.

▲ It is believed that revenues from the cocoa trade contributed to funding the armed conflict in the Ivory Coast.

Global Witness Report
Hot Chocolate: How Cocoa Fuelled the Conflict in Cote d'Ivoire

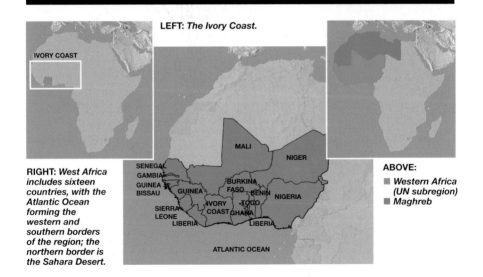

LEFT: *The Ivory Coast.*

RIGHT: *West Africa includes sixteen countries, with the Atlantic Ocean forming the western and southern borders of the region; the northern border is the Sahara Desert.*

ABOVE:
■ *Western Africa (UN subregion)*
■ *Maghreb*

IVORY COAST

MALI
NIGER
SENEGAL
GAMBIA
GUINEA
BISSAU
GUINEA
BURKINA
FASO
BENIN
NIGERIA
SIERRA
LEONE
IVORY
COAST
TOGO
GHANA
LIBERIA
LIBERIA
ATLANTIC OCEAN

Children are trafficked from the neighbouring counties of Mali and Burkina Faso, or are from other parts of the Ivory Coast. They are isolated from their families and vulnerable to abuse. They are alone.

CONDITIONS FACING TRAFFICKED CHILDREN

Trafficked children are often:
◢ Forced to carry excruciatingly heavy loads
◢ Forced to work with dangerous machetes, resulting in serious injury
◢ Exposed to dangerous pesticides
◢ Given no education
◢ Undernourished
◢ Far from home and frightened.

In April 2001, Humphrey Hawksley produced a report for the BBC exposing the problem of human trafficking to the Ivory Coast. He found children imprisoned on farms, beaten if they tried to escape, some not even eleven years old. The going rate for these children was around £15.

'When you eat chocolate, you eat my flesh.'

A BOY, ELEVEN, TRAFFICKED INTO THE IVORY COAST TO WORK ON A COCOA PLANTATION, SEE *SLAVERY: A GLOBAL INVESTIGATION,* WWW.TRUEVISIONTV.COM

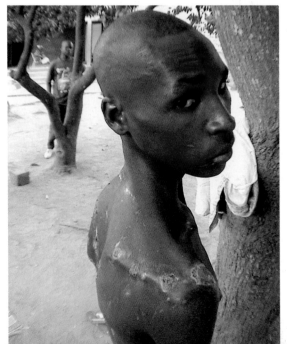

A boy, eleven, trafficked into the Ivory Coast to work on a cocoa plantation. From the slavery film Slavery: A Global Investigation *by Brian Woods, TrueVision, 2001.*

'From what the chocolate makers had told me I thought that finding child labour would be difficult. But just along the main road to Sinfra, we turned into a village, drove down a dirt track, past a cocoa plantation and saw gangs of children coming towards us. They wore grubby, torn T-shirts and carried machetes, their heads hung in confusion. The oldest was thirteen and the youngest was six or seven, kept in line by a 'slave-master' with a bicycle who was only fifteen.'

HUMPHREY HAWKSLEY

Hawksley reported: 'Mali's Save the Children Fund [www.savethechildren.org.uk] Director, Salia Kante, has a message for shoppers… think about what you are buying. "People who are drinking cocoa or coffee are drinking their blood," he said. "It is the blood of young children carrying six kilograms of cocoa sacks so heavy that they have wounds all over their shoulders. It's really pitiful to see."'

BBC

After the shockwaves sent out by his first report, Humphrey Hawksley revisited the Ivory Coast in 2007 and found the situation had not improved.

'Millions of pounds are meant to be being spent on stopping child labour and trafficking. But travelling deeper and deeper into the cocoa belt, I saw very little evidence. No electricity. No drainage, and child after child, machete in hand and scars on legs.

Multinational corporations stand accused of taking huge profit while those who farm their raw products become poorer.'

HUMPHREY HAWKSLEY

Some children are kidnapped, but others are sent away or sold by parents or relatives. Shocking as it may seem that parents should put their own children at risk, many believe that they are sending them to a better life, that they will have the chance to earn some money. But that money is all too often kept by the exploiters.

In West Africa there is a tradition of children going to work with members of the extended family. Around 284,000 children work on cocoa farms there, 200,000 on the Ivory Coast, many of them willingly. It is seen as a way of climbing out of poverty and acquiring a skill. Sometimes a child goes to work with a relative in the hope of earning money to pay school fees.

Cultivating cocoa requires hard labour.

This is a tradition with a long history, and parents living in severe poverty might see it as their duty to give this opportunity to their children. It is surely, they feel, better than staying on a small subsistence farm with no prospects and so little food. Sadly, the practice of sending children away to work is one that traffickers are all too keen to exploit.

So, a relative or member of the community, or someone who claims to be distantly related, might arrive in town after time away, offering an education or an apprenticeship, or a good job in the Ivory Coast. This is unlikely to sound suspicious to parents. In fact, they may have worked on a cocoa farm themselves and emerged unscathed.

Madame Tigana, the Director of the Consortium Amidef/Denbayuman, an NGO that deals with trafficked children in Sikasso, Mali explains the situation:

'Even family members… will say they [the children] must go. On the way, everything that the trafficker says to the child is aimed at keeping the child excited: "These people pay very well, good food is everywhere – meat, chicken, coca-cola"… So the child is very happy to go to Ivory Coast. From the moment that they leave, they feel that they have gained something.'

But, she says: 'Once the children have crossed the border, they see that they are completely alone. They are then taken to a warehouse and sleep there and the people who brought them disappear…

There are many children in this warehouse… sometimes more than 100… Now the planters come and see the warehouse owner and negotiate the price of the children… the children themselves have heard it… They told us that they themselves have heard: "I cannot pay 75000 CFA (£75), lower the price."… In this way, children are sold… The children are then taken directly to the plantation. Once they have gotten to the plantation, it is a catastrophe.'

INTERNATIONAL LABOR RIGHTS FORUM (ILRF),
www.laborrights.org

> 'The fear I felt was like heavy rocks piled up on top of me. And there was no way out, no way away. I'd seen... other slaves who dared to try and run away. They were whipped until what little flesh there was left on their backs hung like strips of meat in the smoke-house.'

UNHEARD VOICES, *COLLECTED BY MALORIE BLACKMAN, CORGI BOOKS, 2007*

This is not a new problem. Slavery on cocoa plantations has a long, shameful heritage. A hundred years ago, *Harper's Magazine* ran a report on cocoa slavery in Sao Thomé and Principe that shocked readers.

'In his progress into the interior, it was no uncommon thing to meet with the caravan's children who had been stolen from their parents. Women too, some of them with babies strapped to their backs, were driven along with whips by brutal overseers. Arrived at the marts, these poor creatures are sold at low rates to plantation holders in the islands of Sao Thomé and Principe".

HENRY NEVINSON'S REPORT ON COCOA SLAVERY FOR *HARPER'S MAGAZINE* 1905, WHEN SAO THOMÉ AND PRINCIPE WERE THE MAIN COCOA-GROWING AREAS

And yet it's still happening. A hundred years on, trafficking is still ruining, and ending, innocent lives. Children are still suffering, and the chocolate industry is still making huge profits.

Cocoa plantations using trafficked child labour continue to cause suffering today.

ANNUAL TURNOVER OF THE TOP TEN CHOCOLATE MANUFACTURERS	
COMPANY	2006 REVENUES *(US$ millions)*
1. Mars, Inc	10,418.3
2. Nestlé SA	7,261.3
3. Ferrero S.p.A.	5,269.6
4. Cadbury Schweppes plc	3,868.2
5. The Hershey Company	3,708.2
6. Barry Callebaut AG	2,911.4
7. Kraft Foods, Inc.	2,875.1
8. Chocoladefabriken Lindt & Sprüngli AG	2,062.5
9. Meiji Seika Kaisha, Ltd.	702.2
10. Russell Stover Candies Inc.	509
TOTAL:	39,585.8

www.computerwire.com

Expressions of outrage and sympathy without action are useless. Becoming aware, informing ourselves, is only the first step. The exploited people, these trafficked children, women and men, need real action. Even these stories of trafficking have reached you at a cost. The people who've done this research have often risked their lives. Investigating trafficking is fraught with danger. French-Canadian journalist, Guy-André Kieffer, was kidnapped on 16 April 2004 and tortured to death after trying to investigate corruption in the Ivory Coast's cocoa industry. This discourages people talking about and reporting the issue.

'National and international journalists and human rights organizations have documented incidents of intimidation and violence against those who investigate or speak out about abuses in the cocoa sector, particularly in the government-held area. Cocoa-sector insiders, journalists and auditors have been targeted. Those responsible for these threats and acts of violence have not been brought to justice. The case of Guy-André Kieffer… is emblematic of this climate of fear and violence. His case is always foremost in the minds of those wanting to speak out, leading to a form of self-censorship which has reinforced the silence and opacity surrounding the cocoa sector.'

GLOBAL WITNESS REPORT, *HOT CHOCOLATE: HOW COCOA FUELLED THE CONFLICT IN COTE D'IVOIRE*

Nevertheless, there are many positive steps that can be taken to raise awareness about the issue of human trafficking.

In the world of industry, the consumer makes the decisions. Not the bosses, not the accountants, but the buyers. If we insist on products that are demonstrably free from human trafficking, if we vote with our money and buy only fairly traded goods, industries will have to react. They will have to guarantee that their products are slave-free.

Two hundred years ago, so many consumers stopped buying sugar until it was guaranteed to be 'slave free' that the industry had to respond. Shopkeepers started advertising in their windows when they sold slave-free sugar. The consumers of the day knew their power – and they used it. And there was nothing the industry could do to stop them.

So if consumers take action to demand that the chocolate industry uses transparent supply chains, independently confirmed as ethical throughout, then the exploiters will be unable to sell their ill-gotten goods to us. We stop supporting trafficking.

On a cold and windy day in March 2007, children from London schools stood outside the headquarters of Nestlé UK in Croydon, holding signs drawing people's attention to the trafficking going on in the chocolate supply chain.

There are more slaves alive today than there were bought, transported and sold in the 450 years of the slave trade. It is the fastest growing global crime – only the illegal arms trade is bigger. Each one of the Croydon schoolchildren represents 5,000 children working in slavery in Africa. Nestlé's slogan is 'Good Food, Good Life'; what they mean is it's a good life for us – but at the expense of the thousands of child slaves on the Ivory Coast. If it was our children or grandchildren in this situation, if one of the Nestlé executives had just one of their children in slavery anywhere, the problem would be sorted out by teatime. We call on them, and other chocolate manufacturers, to make their products slave-free.

STOP THE TRAFFIK Chocolate Campaign, held outside Nestlé headquarters, Croydon, UK.

Until now, the chocolate industry has failed to respond with significant change. They have been asked to sign up to the Traffik-free pledge.

THE TRAFFIK-FREE PLEDGE

If the chocolate industry agrees to this pledge, it agrees to:

1. **Provide transparency in the cocoa supply chain to farm level.**
   We will provide our customers with detailed information about the origins of our cocoa beans and will support the establishment of systems that can map in any given growing season all the farms, production sites and cooperatives from which we may have sourced cocoa beans. Additionally, we will publish and make publicly available full information on any payments made to government entities in cocoa-producing countries.

2. **Commit to sourcing exclusively from farms and cooperatives which respect the core ILO labour standards,** and pay a price adequate for those producers to meet these standards. We agree to certification by third-party auditors which is independent from our companies to ensure that core labour standards are upheld by our producers and within our supply chains.

3. **Pay farmers a fair and adequate price for the cocoa we purchase.**
   'Fair and adequate' is defined as a price that exceeds the costs of production and that allows farmers to meet the basic human needs of their families and workers, including adequate nutrition, shelter, medical care, and primary education.

4. We will implement – or maintain – as the case may be, the following **structural practices so as to ensure farmers a consistently better price:** simplifying our supply chain, working with cooperatives, encouraging cooperatization, providing more market information to farmers and committing to long-term trade relationships with cocoa producers.

5. **Support the drafting and enforcement of national and international laws that prohibit human trafficking, debt bondage and the other worst forms of child labour** (in accordance with ILO Convention 182).

6. **Finance the rehabilitation, reintegration and education of children** who have been exploited by the worst forms of child labour (as defined by ILO Convention 182) on cocoa farms, both in the growing countries and labour exporting countries, through direct support to local and international development organizations with an expertise in child rights, unless you are already committed to 100% Fairtrade Certified sourcing of cocoa.

'When Cadbury's and Hershey, and Mars and Lindt and Nestlé and all of the others, produce chocolate that is traffick free, you can be sure they they will be the first to put a little mark on those bars telling us that. If a chocolate bar doesn't say it's traffick free; if it doesn't say it's fairly traded it's just not. It's as simple as that.'

STEVE CHALKE, FOUNDER OF STOP THE TRAFFIK

Reports by Humphrey Hawksley, Brian Woods (who recorded the child whose words open this chapter), and Knight Ridder of the *New York Times* have caused outrage across the globe. But what practical action has taken place?

One politician in the US, Eliot Engel, decided to add an amendment to an agriculture bill passing through the American Congress, calling for a scheme where chocolate in America would have to carry the stamp 'free of child slave labour'.

As soon as the chocolate industry found out, it lobbied hard to get this stopped. So instead of making a law ensuring industry would stop using forced child labour, it was agreed that this should be voluntary.

Engel, working with Senator Tom Harkin, persuaded industry to agree to 'The Harkin Engel Protocol'. It promised that industry would act to wipe out the worst exploitation, including trafficking from the farms from which they bought cocoa, by July 2005. The protocol stated:

'Industry, in partnership with other major stakeholders, will develop and implement credible, mutually acceptable, voluntary, industry-wide standards of public certification, consistent with applicable federal law, that cocoa beans and their derivative products have been grown and/or processed without any of the worst forms of child labour.'

In other words, the chocolate industry promised to ensure that only farms which were certified as free from trafficked labour could supply the cocoa that makes our chocolate.

'That deadline came and went and we were very unhappy.'

ELIOT ENGEL, US POLITICIAN

Without industry's fulfilment of this promise, slavery will never be eradicated from the cocoa industry.

The chocolate industry was given the deadline of 1 July 2008 to keep its promise. In London, a spokeswoman for the Biscuit, Cake, Chocolate and Confectionery Association has said she believed the industry was on target to keep its promise: 'We are firmly committed to creating a supply chain free from the worst forms of child labour and forced labour.'

But the deadline has passed. And, as Humphrey Hawksley states: 'thousands of children continue to work on the cocoa farms – the impoverished end of a business chain that earns billions of pounds a year.'

We are still waiting.

> **'The chocolate industry can give us chocolate that is sugar-free, fat-free, nut-free and additive-free... so why can't they proudly tell us it's slave-free as well?'**
>
> RUTH DEARNLEY, CEO OF STOP THE TRAFFIK

OTHER INDUSTRIES

Sadly, chocolate is just one of many industries blighted by trafficking. The abuses endured on cocoa plantations are being dealt out with similar cruelty in many other trades: tea, coffee, cotton, even mobile phones.

To the children whose backs are stripped, who sweat and cry and bleed, it makes no difference. Chocolate, coffee, cotton – life is the same.

We need to find out whether what we buy has a history, whether that history is exploiting vulnerable people.

One of the factors that makes a product's history hard to see is globalization. Globalization, for all its benefits, allows for pockets of secrecy to develop in supply chains. With industries operating on a massive, global scale, it is even easier for traffickers who deal in forced labour to infiltrate the process of supplying goods to those industries, while going unnoticed by the consumer.

So when we walk round a supermarket and spot a bargain, how can we know whether it is cheap only because somebody hasn't been paid for helping to produce it?

Consumers have a choice. It may be the choice between grabbing a bargain, or spending a little more knowing that the goods are traffik-free. But it is a significant choice.

> **'Free yourself from the slavery of tea and coffee.'**
>
> WILLIAM COBBETT (1763–1835), *POLITICAL ACTIVIST WHO CHAMPIONED THE RIGHTS OF FARM LABOURERS*

COTTON AND CLOTHING

> There were the girls and their mothers working at their sewing,
> or their shoe-binding, or their trimming, or their waistcoat making, day
> and night and night and day, and not more than able to keep body and
> soul together... – often not so much.

CHARLES DICKENS, *LITTLE DORRIT*

Exploitation is not new. Henry Nevinson's report of 1905 shows that trafficking is an age-old problem. And Dickens' pleas for social justice in the nineteenth century show that humanity has always exploited its poor.

In the cotton industry, girls are particularly at risk. Being both children and female, they are the most 'disposable'.

'Child labour in the production of cottonseed in India, particularly in the state of Andhra Pradesh, has been extremely widespread. Children, especially girls, are employed by farmers in order to cut costs, as they are paid well below the minimum wage and the wages paid to adult workers. The child workers are often in a state of debt bondage since their employers pay an advance to the children's parents and then they must work to meet the amount paid.

The children generally work at least nine hours a day, but during the winter, they often work up to twelve hours a day. Pesticides used during production cause health problems for the children and they report experiencing headaches, weakness, disorientation, convulsions and respiratory problems and the long-term effects of exposure to toxic chemicals has not been measured.

Migrant child laborers, who often come from farms where their parents do not own sufficient land to earn a living income, are especially at risk for labour abuses. Multinational corporations such as Monsanto and Bayer are major purchasers of cottonseeds from this region. While the companies have started to take action to address the concerns of workers and civil society, there is still much more work to be done to end child labour in the industry.'

INTERNATIONAL LABOR RIGHTS FORUM (ILRF)

Label of clothing produced in India.

Imagine a friend, a cousin, a sister, a daughter. Imagine her having to work twelve-hour days, dizzy, wheezing, struggling to focus, struggling to breathe. That's the reality for many girls. All to make the cheap cotton T-shirt you bought without thinking twice. Let's start. Let's start thinking twice.

Today, we have a choice. We can despair that exploitation is an age-old problem, that human nature never changes – and then do nothing. Or you can feel determined to be part of the generation that exposes trafficking and brings it to its knees. You can act.

A traffick-free lifestyle is worth working at. Make one choice at a time. And it won't be just your life that is changed.

The hidden faces of today's slaves were represented in an episode of the BBC science-fiction drama *Doctor Who*, in which the Doctor's assistant, Donna, an ordinary twenty-first-century woman, expresses disgust at a futuristic scenario of slave-labour:

> *Donna: 'A great big empire built on slavery!'*
> *Doctor: 'It's not so different from your own time.'*
> *Donna: 'Oi, I haven't got slaves!'*
> *Doctor: 'Who do you think made your clothes?'*

BBC *DOCTOR WHO* SERIES 4, EPISODE 3: "PLANET OF THE OOD", BY KEITH TEMPLE, 2008. WWW.BBC.CO.UK/DOCTORWHO/S4/EPISODES/S4_03

You can learn more about cotton production and what you can do to help end exploitation by going to:

www.laborrights.org/stop-child-labor/cottoncampaign

The globalization of supply chains means companies can use cheap labour in developing countries while still running their company in the West.

In theory this gives developing countries new economic opportunities.

But in reality if they start raising their wages, the company can remove its employment and leave behind economic crisis. So there is a strong incentive to keep wages low – and this can often mean using trafficked workers.

What is worse, many companies today are run from the other side of the world, by people ignorant of the conditions of workers and who, even when they are aware, struggle to effect changes from afar.

Out of sight, out of mind.

THE CASE OF NIKE

Nike realized in the 1970s that most high-tech sports shoes in the US were made in the US, so if they sourced their shoes from low-wage countries in Asia, they would have a competitive advantage. By 2004 Nike's products were made in fifty-one countries, employing more than 600,000 staff. Production kept shifting to find lower-wage workers who could still supply quality. Although there were 600,000 staff, only 24,291 were employed directly, reducing the control Nike had on the labour conditions they were working under.

Like others in the clothing industry, Nike enters into short-term contracts with suppliers, so control of labour conditions is weakened even further. In the 1990s, there was a series of labour scandals including child labour in Cambodia, China, Indonesia and Vietnam. This was reported in a well-publicised article on the front page of the *New York Times* on 8 November 1997, which stated that labourers made only eighty pence a week – half of what it costs to live. In 1998, Philip Knight, the Nike founder admitted: 'The Nike product has become synonymous with slave wages, forced overtime, and arbitrary abuse.'

In response to this, Nike has developed a code of conduct, trains its staff and regularly audits its factories. But because of the global nature of its supply chain, and the fact that Nike does not directly employ most of the people making its products, it is a huge task to keep trafficked and abused labour out of the supply chain.

The more contact Nike has directly with the factory, the more it can be sure that the factory is complying with the code of conduct, but the nature of a globalized supply chain makes this a tremendous challenge.

NIKE IS A COMPANY WHICH IS COMMITTED TO CHANGE.

But when other companies fail to commit to this kind of intervention, the exploitation continues.

There is a brilliant scene in Michael Moore's documentary *The Big One,* where Philip Knight, Founder and former CEO of Nike, which has become notorious for its abuse of workers overseas, invites Moore to talk with him. So Moore goes in to meet with Knight bearing a gift – two first-class tickets to Indonesia. And he invites Knight to fly to Indonesia and simply walk through his factories. Phil busts out laughing and shakes his head, 'No, no, not a chance.' Moore tells him that he just wants to walk through and check out the operation, and then asks, 'Have you ever been to see your factories where your shoes are made? Have you ever been to Indonesia?' Knight says, 'No, and I am not going to go.'

> 'These are the layers of separation that allow injustice to happen. It's not that people are malicious. I do not think we are naturally able to hurt each other. Even Philip Knight seems like too nice of a guy for that. But we keep ourselves at a safe distance.'

SHANE CLAIBORNE,
'THE IRRESISTIBLE REVOLUTION', ZONDERVAN, 2006

MOBILES

> 'You can't even be certain that the cell you have in your pocket wasn't made with slave labour.'

AIDAN MCQUADE,
DIRECTOR OF ANTI-SLAVERY INTERNATIONAL, LONDON

One of the main components within a mobile phone is made from the super-conductor coltan.

About 80% of coltan is supplied by the eastern part of the Democratic Republic of Congo – a country that has been torn apart by civil war and competing factions. It is also a place where trafficking and forced labour are rife (*www.securitymanagement.com*).

CARPETS

The handmade carpet industry exploits nearly 300,000 children in South Asia and is a major 'employer' of child labour.

Children aged four to fourteen are kidnapped or trafficked, sold into debt bondage or forced labour. They suffer from malnutrition, impaired vision and deformities from sitting long hours in cramped loom sheds, as well as from respiratory diseases from inhaling wool fibres, with wounds from using sharp tools.

Rugs are among South Asia's top export products and a high-employment sector for the poor. If child exploitation is normal in a country's principal industry, there is little chance to break the cycle of extreme poverty.

Learn more to end this abuse: Rugmark Foundation (www.rugmark.org).

FAIRTRADE

Fairtrade is based on four principles:

1. Pay a reasonable price to farmers that at least covers the cost of production and basic living costs.

2. Pay a premium that the farmers have to invest in their community.

3. Ensure that it is possible for farmers to be paid an advance to meet costs.

4. Contracts are long-term, which allows for planning and stability.

ROUGH GUIDE TO ETHICAL LIVING

FAIRTRADE FACTS

▲ During Easter 2008, a popular London newspaper reported that the sale of Fairtrade Easter Eggs in the UK had risen by 20%.

▲ The Fairtrade Foundation reported that 2007 saw an increase of estimated retail sales of Fairtrade products to £493 million.

▲ Fairtrade bananas are the best-selling fair trade product with sales topping £150 million, an increase of 130% in 2007 over the previous year.

▲ One in four bananas sold are now Fairtrade and we eat three million fair trade bananas a day.

▲ Fairtrade coffee sales rose 24% to over £117 million in 2007.

▲ Items made with Fairtrade certified cotton increased from over half a million to just under 9.5 million units in 2007.

▲ Fairtrade tea rose 24% to just over £30 million. And recent commercial developments mean Fairtrade tea should account for a tenth of tea sold in the UK by the end of 2008.

▲ In 2007 the real volumes (by weight or number) of produce more than doubled over 2006: great news for the producers whose Fairtrade premiums are based on these volumes.

For more information, see www.fairtrade.org.uk

FAIRTADE V. FREETRADE

Free trade is a market model in which the trade of goods and services between or within countries flows unaffected by externally imposed requirements.

Fairtrade is an externally imposed set of guidelines providing a better deal for farmers and farm workers, while ensuring that produce is traffik-free.

QUESTIONS RAISED

In 2008 the Adam Smith Institute released a controversial report claiming that Fairtrade does not successfully fulfil its aims. The report claimed:

◢ That paying farmers for their produce sustains uncompetitive farming methods rather than encouraging modern techniques

◢ That payment structures put in place by the Fairtrade Foundation, which operates the Fairtrade label, unintentionally encourage farms in developing countries to take on labourers only during harvest time rather than employing them full-time

◢ That a fraction of the Fairtrade premium paid by consumers actually reaches the producer, while retailers pocket the rest

◢ That Fairtrade distorts the market by keeping the price high.

BRITISH NEWSPAPER, *THE DAILY TELEGRAPH*

ANSWERS OFFERED

Promoters of free trade in the developing world are often aiming to capture a larger share of these developing countries' markets. Their desire is to pre-empt the emergence of possible competitors in the developing world by maintaining the status quo – which means massive discrepancies between company profits and ground-level wages, the chasm between rich and poor.

Fairtrade, on the other hand, undeniably helps thousands of poor people around the world.

To argue that Fairtrade does not work for the poorest of the poor, and so should not be done, is like saying that formal schooling does not work for the poorest because they have to work to get food – and then go on to conclude that formal schooling is never a good idea.

We need to expand the number of cooperatives into as many areas as possible to help the poorest – but this is not an argument against Fairtrade.

Fairtrade does not distort the market any more than it is already distorted. The market is already distorted to keep prices low. For instance, for cocoa there are ten main exporters and over 600,000 farms in the Ivory Coast: all the market power is with the exporters. It is in their interests to keep cocoa prices low – which in turn denies farmers a fair wage.

Fairtrade cooperatives make the monitoring of standards much easier, and also help to overcome the power inequality of the market, giving bargaining power to farmers.

Fairtrade helps with market information: it is the cooperative that negotiates the price, instead of one farmer, who, in the case of cocoa in the Ivory Coast, gets one visit from a trader, or 'pisteur', and has to take or leave the price, powerless to negotiate.

Free trade does not help to create sustainable production – it does not help farmers long term in the way that Fairtrade does.

In the aftermath of colonialism, many developing world economies switched from subsistence agriculture to cash crops to serve Europe. Unfortunately, these cash crops are subject to wide fluctuations in price, as they are traded on the commodities market.

This instability of price means that farmers are not sure of what the future holds and also are not certain that their income will even cover expenses.

Fairtrade is an answer to these problems: a guaranteed minimum price creates the possibility of sustainable production, and counterbalances the inequalities in what was never 'free' trade in the first place.

ETHICAL TRADE

A guide to Ethical Trade from www.ethicaltrade.org:

'Ethical trade' can be an umbrella term for all types of business practices that promote more socially and/or environmentally responsible trade.

Some, including the Ethical Trade Initiative (ETI), use the term in a narrower sense, referring to the labour practices in a company's supply chain, i.e. the assumption of responsibility by a company for the labour and human rights practices within its supply chain.

A code of practice – or code of conduct – is a set of standards/rules for ethical behaviour. This refers to a code adopted by a company which sets out minimum labour standards that they expect suppliers and sub-contractors to meet.

There are now hundreds of such codes in existence. These codes differ significantly in terms of what labour standards they contain, who is involved in developing and managing them, and how they are being monitored and implemented.

Increasingly, those involved in ethical trade, including Ethical Trade Initiative, recognize International Labour Organization (ILO) standards as an international benchmark for labour codes.

A full list of ILO conventions and recommendations can be found at www.ilo.org.

But we need to keep asking: who verifies these codes? Are they being *independently* checked? If not, can we really trust a company to claim that its own practices are ethical?

Remember, the consumer is king. What we say, goes. If enough of us ask, there will have to be answers.

So, use your power to support ethical initiatives. Wherever possible, buy Fairtrade goods. It's an easy and effective way to show your support for ethical working conditions – free from the scourge of trafficking.

To repeat the words of Mali's Save the Children Fund Director, Salia Kante:

THINK ABOUT WHAT YOU ARE BUYING

WAYS TO BUY FREEDOM

TAKE THIS SHOPPING LIST WITH YOUR QUESTION LIST.

◢ **Can I get this product Fairtrade?**

◢ **Which retailers on my high street promote Fairtrade and ethically produced goods?**

◢ **Could my town be a Fairtrade town?**

◢ **If it's cheap, what was the human cost?**

◢ **If it's organic, does that mean it's traffick-free?**

See: www.fairtrade.org.uk/get_involved/campaigns/fairtrade_towns.

Be inspired by the first Fairtrade town, Garstang in Lancashire, UK: www.garstangfairtrade.org.uk.

DID YOU KNOW, YOU CAN NOW BUY:

◢ Fairtrade **chocolate** (see our Good Chocolate Guide)

◢ Fairtrade **sugar, honey, biscuits, sweet**s

◢ Fairtrade **beer** – see www.fairtradebeer.com

◢ Fairtrade **bananas** (from most supermarkets), other **fruits** and **juices**

◢ Fairtrade **coffee** and **tea**, including **green tea** and **white tea** (from most supermarkets)

◢ Fairtrade **cereals, cereal bars, cakes**

◢ Fairtrade cotton clothes including **T-shirts** and **jeans**

◢ Fairtrade **shoes** and **kids' clothing**

◢ Fairtrade **flowers**

… and lots more!

It's always worth checking online for Fairtrade and ethically produced options. Visit www.fairtrade.org.uk/products/retail_products for more information.

> **'Just a spoonful of sugar makes the medicine go down…'**
>
> **MARY POPPINS**

A spoonful of sugar *not* taken by an estimated 300,000 people in Great Britain over 200 years ago in protest against the use of slave labour in the production of sugar had a powerful effect.

So powerful, in fact, that those retailers previously selling sugar tainted by slavery were quickly sourcing alternative suppliers, and pasting up notices in their shops declaring their sugar to be slave free.

If we take the same stand, and buy only Fairtrade chocolate, the chocolate industry will have to respond in the same way as the sugar industry did 200 years ago. It will have to cut its ties to slavery.

'Our youngest abolitionists… received their spoonful of sugar via a bar of Fairtrade chocolate when they met for their Children's Council in Levin [New Zealand].

Their theme for the weekend was "freedom" and they spent time learning about historical slavery and present-day trafficking, and what it means to be free or not free.

The children have also signed postcards addressed to Members of Parliament, expressing their concerns and asking for action to be taken. They are especially asking for Parliament to encourage all manufacturers of chocolate to make sure their cocoa source is not tainted in any way by slavery.'

CHRIS FRAZER, SOCIAL JUSTICE ADVOCATE
SALVATION ARMY, NEW ZEALAND

Fairtrade coffee and chocolate.

STOP THE SHOPPING

Why not give this coupon to the retailer when you pay for your chocolate? Carry the coupons around with you and hand one in every time you buy chocolate. Let chocolate retailers know why you are buying Fairtrade chocolate and encourage them to sign the pledge, join the campaign and provide chocolate that is TRAFFICK FREE.

Download the STOP THE TRAFFIK coupon at www.stopthetraffik.org/getinvolved/act/chocolate/chocation.

CHAPTER 6

'I have heard their groans and sighs, and seen their tears, and I would give every drop of blood in my veins to set them free.'

HARRIET TUBMAN (1820–1913),
ESCAPED-SLAVE-TURNED-ABOLITIONIST

CHOCOLATE
CAMPAIGN

'They have bled. I have wept.
We must act.'

A teacher attended a conference and heard about STOP THE TRAFFIK. She was shocked at the scale and brutality of human trafficking, and decided to tell her class about it in a lesson.

A little girl sat open-mouthed as she heard about children on cocoa farms treated like slaves. She went home and told her family all about it. Her grandmother, who happened to be a Baroness in the House of Lords, listened in horror. She got in touch with the STOP THE TRAFFIK organization, and, with one of her colleagues, took the Chocolate Campaign to Parliament.

The chocolate industry heard about this. It was not happy about its links to trafficking being exposed so publicly, so it asked to meet with these women. The women have since reported that the chocolate industry could not reasonably answer any of their questions. The industry was put on the spot – and all because a little girl listened to her teacher talking about trafficking.

This is how campaigning works. All it takes is one person to take one simple action. That action sets in motion a train of events, and big things start to happen.

FACTS TO MAKE YOU ACT

These facts show how trafficking causes severe damage to the health of individuals – and whole communities:

◢ **Trafficked sex workers are vulnerable to contracting HIV/AIDS, sexually transmitted diseases (STDs), pelvic inflammatory disease, hepatitis and tuberculosis. It has been reported that 80% of sex workers who sought help from the Prostitution Emergency Reporting Centre 'were found to have suffered from diseases, including venereal diseases, mental illness and other symptoms due to forced and frequent sex'.**

Korea Times, 16 November 2004

◢ **'The health implications of sex trafficking extend not only to its victims, but also to the general public... sex trafficking is aiding the global dispersion of HIV subtypes.**

US State Department

MAKONEN GETU 'Human Trafficking and Development: The Role of Microfinance' in *Transformation*, Vol.23, 3 July 2006

ANDREA'S STORY

Andrea, thirty-four, who was trafficked as a sex worker, has suffered from many health problems due to the work she was forced to do – she is now determined to take action so that others avoid her experience:

'I was in love. My "prince charming" promised me a better life in Holland. I could leave behind a life of poverty and family problems. But I couldn't fathom that I would be exploited by a criminal network. My "prince" was a monster. And I lived a nightmare. I had to work in a cheap brothel in Germany near the Dutch border. I had terrible problems with STDs. I also worked in a fancy mansion close to Amsterdam, with drugs, alcohol and wealthy clients. My body, my soul… my life belonged to a group of criminals who blackmailed me, threatened to kill me and were always saying they could harm my family back home.

Now that I have managed to escape to Brazil I want everybody to know about what happened to me so that no other human being becomes a victim of trafficking.'

ANDREA, INTERVIEWED BY THE UNODC REGIONAL OFFICE IN BRAZIL
PUBLISHED IN *HUMAN TRAFFICKING: AN OVERVIEW*, UN (2008)

'I can't think of anything more selfish than to pretend someone else isn't a human too.'

HOLLYOAKS STAR JAKE HENDRIKS
(KIERON HOBBS)

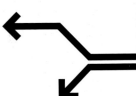

FATHER SHAY CULLEN'S STORY

Father Shay Cullen has devoted his life to fighting trafficking. People like Shay show tremendous courage and commitment in combatting this issue. For him, it is his vocation in life. But he recognized that a group is stronger than an individual – and this led him to set up the Preda Foundation in the Philippines.

He tells of one of his many encounters with traffickers:

'When I take a walk in the Luneta, the mall, walk the streets in Makati or Pasay or even in Malate Park, sooner or later a pimp will sidle up and, mistaking me for a tourist say, "Want a girl, Joe?"

I look disinterested and ignore the pimp.

Then he says with a broad smile, "Oh! Maybe a boy, I know lots of nice young boys, clean, friendly, you want?"

Again I look away, pulling a face of disinterested disgust, hardly saying a word.

The pimp looks puzzled for a moment and then says, "You like them young, Joe? No problem, I can get you twelve, thirteen, fourteen year old, you want? You can do any thing you like, F--- them, anything. A thousand pesos, two thousand for a virgin and for the pimp five hundred."

I ask him, "Are you the pimp?"

"Yes, that me," he replies. "I can get them now, they are over there." He points to a pillar holding up the Department of Tourism building where, two small children had emerged from the shadows and were caught in the bright lights.

Sometimes I played along with his offer, asking more questions and the whole world of child sexual slavery came spilling out. Some people won't believe it happens so casually, with no fear of police either. That is why I decided to bring along a miniature video recorder and record the offers of child sex, which is in itself a crime that could get a pimp a sentence of eight years in jail.

One day, on the street in a nightclub area with my Filipino friend, I was offered children for sex. "Where are they?" I asked.

"I will show you," the pimp said and we got into a taxi and were brought to a back street. We were shown into a room where there were about eighteen young girls. This was a child brothel.

The manager gushed with excitement and glee at the prospect of a sale.

"This is Maria, she is fourteen and you can have all night long for P2500. This other one is Judith, fifteen, P2000 only. If you want a young virgin, she will cost you P3000, but you will have to come back, they are very scarce nowadays," he said, as if talking about a rare fruit that spoils easily.

Then he sent out for his best human merchandise, a small girl who was sleeping after entertaining her last customer in an upstairs room.

She looked frail and exhausted. I was witnessing chained slavery, hardly any different from that of the slave sales of the last century. We both made our excuses and left. I had my miniature video camera running and the batteries had not run out as had happened on previous occasions.

Later, we realized that it was too dangerous for us to try and rescue the children ourselves and I wrote up the report giving the names of the suspects, or their aliases, and the address that we had carefully noted.

I sent it to high police officials in the Department of the Interior, offering to cooperate and hoping they would call and discuss the crime we witnessed, identify the suspects, give a statement and ask for the videotape.

But nine months later, nothing. Silence total and absolute. The children are still in that brothel and many more like it.

Last week, I was on my way to take a walk in the Luneta where I had been previously offered children – as will happen to any male tourist if he risks hanging about the skating rink at night in front of the Department of Tourism building or other haunts of pimps selling children.

I called Director Santiago Toledo and asked for his assistance, explaining I was working with the Presidential Committee for the Protection of Children. He referred me at once to the National Bureau of Investigation (NBI) anti-paedophile unit.

I went to the office of the NBI Commander with my companion and I explained what was going on, and how easy it would be to catch a notorious pimp if an NBI agent came with me playing the role of guide.

But it was not to be. The attorney reasoned that standing around in the park would be instigation – and that would never do. No such ploy or tactic could be used.

So the trafficking in children goes on undisturbed by NBI surveillance or the like. I wonder how the anti-narcotics agents are able to mount buy-bust operations with regular success and not be cited for instigation.

Not far from the commander's window, a short drive away, small children are still being offered as child prostitutes at the tender ages of twelve and even less.

Paedophile paradise is well protected and it seems that the paedophiles, local and foreign, get away with unspeakable crimes, while those who should and could do much, seem to do so little.'

FATHER SHAY CULLEN, PREDA HOME FOR CHILDREN,
UPPER KALAKLAN, OLONGAPO CITY, PHILIPPINES (www.preda.org)

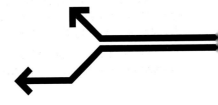

Father Shay Cullen, founder of the Preda Foundation, with children. These children have been rescued from abusers and sex bars where they were trafficked into sex slavery. Local government officials arrange pay-offs to parents from paedophiles and traffickers.

It is important to note here that Father Shay, who already took a risk by investigating this pimp, knew his limits. He said, 'we realized that it was too dangerous for us to try and rescue the children ourselves.'

It is not worth getting into dangerous situations with traffickers. Traffickers are ruthless. But by working as a team with STOP THE TRAFFIK and its sister organizations such as the Preda Foundation, we can lobby the authorities to start taking action that will really work – long term. Father Shay's story has not ended. The authorities did nothing. But by raising awareness and demanding justice, this inertia will have to end. We need visionaries. But we also need teams, and communities, to put that vision into action.

'All that is necessary for the triumph of evil is for good men to do nothing.'

EDMUND BURKE (1729–97)

Minors can recover from the trauma of emotional pain by releasing it in the therapy room for emotional expression therapy with the help of a Preda Foundation therapist. This helps to empower them so that they can testify against their abusers.

TAKING ACTION
PROJECTS

Organizations support a wide range of anti-trafficking projects. The following gives a flavour of the range of work undertaken by STOP THE TRAFFIK:

▲ **European Hotline:** Helping the European Union (EU) Parliament work towards a ground-breaking single phone number to be used throughout Europe. This is currently the subject of a feasibility study in the hope that the hotline can be adopted by all the EU member states.

▲ **'Traffik-Free' chocolate:** Working towards the elimination of people trafficking in cocoa products. The industry is slowly limping in the right direction. We aim to drive it forward through visits to key production sites and cocoa agencies, as well as strengthen our case through presentations and further research.

▲ **United Nations:** STOP THE TRAFFIK has been appointed Special Adviser On Community Action Against People Trafficking, holding meetings in Vienna to develop community resources worldwide.

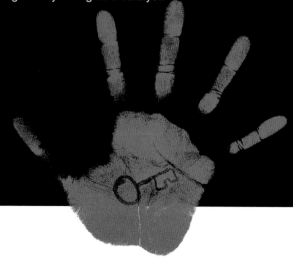

- ▲ **Police, immigration and customs** are already using awareness leaflets. We are also developing training materials and films to be used by the authorities.

- ▲ **ACT/s: Active Communities against Trafficking in the sex industry**: We are mobilzing communities to engage with local authorities and law enforcement agencies to raise awareness of sex trafficking, map sex trafficking in their area, and provide information to local police forces.

- ▲ **Business Travellers against Human Trafficking**. This is a special ACT/s group aimed at business travellers. The website www. businesstravellers.org gives business travellers information about human trafficking and a simple low-key way to report anything they might see through the website. STOP THE TRAFFIK staff will then report to the police any relevant information.

- ▲ **Government lobbying and advocacy** has led to parliamentary debates and pressure on improved legislation. STOP THE TRAFFIK presses for improved legislation and protection for the victims of sex trafficking and the elimination of trafficking in consumer goods and supply chains.

- ▲ **STOP THE TRAFFIK** community membership and action has been welcomed by law enforcement as a vital source of intelligence in the fight against people traffickers, building regional networks and materials to educate and empower grassroots communities.

- ▲ **Our award-winning website** and social networking have reached organizations in over fifty countries. We aim to extend global awareness through downloadable information, films and resources and by passing on vital information to partners as a 'shop window' for the campaign.

- ▲ **Many of the 1,000 member organizations** undertake their own anti-people trafficking work; STOP THE TRAFFIK aids this process through networking, resourcing and by acting as a catalyst.

LEVELS OF ACTION

As the sheer range of the work demonstrates, there are different levels of action needed to combat trafficking. All work together, on different scales, to help tackle this crime. These are:

◢ Global action

◢ National action

◢ Community action

◢ Individual action.

You've seen how a teacher telling a little girl about trafficking led to parliament challenging the chocolate industry. Small actions can lead to big things. Just imagine what can happen when plenty of individuals take small actions.

One person jumping up and down won't cause a tidal wave. But if everyone jumps together, the effect is impossible to ignore. Let's start jumping together and engulf the world with this message: let's STOP THE TRAFFIK.

And that's when big things will start to happen.

The Freedom Wall created using graffiti at Gregg School in Southampton, UK.

GLOBAL ACTION

Trafficking is an international issue. With the United Nations Global Initiative to Fight Human Trafficking (UN.GIFT), STOP THE TRAFFIK aims to raise awareness about trafficking across the globe.

EDUCATION

One example of this is when UN.GIFT joined with STOP THE TRAFFIK in launching a worldwide cartoon competition. Educating young people on the issue is a crucial step in empowering them with the knowledge to understand the true nature of the crime, and reduce the risk of young people from falling prey to potential traffickers. The winning entry from Zane Applegate, who is from Enfield Academy in the UK, will be used in future UN.GIFT publications to raise young people's awareness on this issue (see next page).

ADVOCACY

Through advocacy we can call on our governments and industries to take action that will make a real difference, long term, on an international scale. This can be achieved through actions that combat both sides of human trafficking: supply (trafficked people and traffickers) and demand (for example, sex buyers and cocoa farm owners).

CATEGORIES OF ACTION

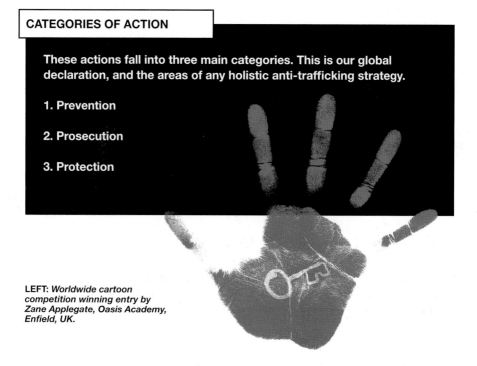

These actions fall into three main categories. This is our global declaration, and the areas of any holistic anti-trafficking strategy.

1. Prevention

2. Prosecution

3. Protection

LEFT: *Worldwide cartoon competition winning entry by Zane Applegate, Oasis Academy, Enfield, UK.*

PREVENTION ◢

Education is vital to prevention. Communities, parents, government officials and police all need to be informed about human trafficking to increase vigilance and put people on their guard against the risks.

Safe migration networks enable migrants to travel legally at less risk from human trafficking. This need not mean an increase in migration but a more open approach, which acknowledges the need for people to move between countries to seek employment, and offers those who do so safer passage – and freedom from exploitation by traffickers.

Poverty is a root cause of human trafficking. In particular, comparative poverty, where people live difficult lives but hear about wealthier communities in other regions, in another city or another country, can cause people to take risky migration decisions. Through the alleviation of poverty and creation of income opportunities, we can empower those people vulnerable to human trafficking to become self-sufficient. And that means they are far less easily lured by the money offered by traffickers.

'... the absence of systematic poverty eradication strategies and the lack of sustained efforts within prevention activities undermine the impact of the entire prevention arsenal.'

UNICEF

One method of tackling poverty is called 'microfinance'. Microfinance institutions such as the Geneva Global and the Center for Community Transformation (CCT) report successful anti-trafficking strategies.

'In countries where ILO works to assist in attaining compliance with core labour standards, such as the [abolition] of forced labour and child labour, microfinance initiatives have played a key role. They help replace family income when a child labourer leaves work and goes to school, provide poor workers with credit to avoid slipping into debt bondage, assist women who are vulnerable to human trafficking and help migrant workers send remittances for income-generating activities.'

ILO, 2005

MICROFINANCE INVOLVES:

◢ Creating employment opportunities for vulnerable people

◢ Promoting sustainable development

◢ Transforming areas susceptible to human trafficking.

This is achieved through:

INCOME GENERATION AND JOB CREATION
Whereas traffickers promise job opportunities in unknown and remote destinations, microfinance offers jobs in familiar and nearby places.

EDUCATION
Microfinance institutions offer loans to poor entrepreneurs to set up community-based schools. This increases the number of schools available. Education and literacy bring hope. Education increases opportunities and arms people with knowledge, which makes them harder for traffickers to exploit.

VOCATIONAL SKILLS TRAINING
Microfinance organizations such as Opportunity International and its partners run youth apprenticeship projects to help young adults gain skills and find jobs. Developing skills, and increasing opportunities and self-worth, makes people less likely to accept work from traffickers.

FAMILY WELL-BEING
By providing education on family planning and child upbringing, microfinance institutions can also help improve the quality of family life. This in turn creates supportive homes. Therefore there is no need to escape; there is no erosion of self-belief from an abusive upbringing. This means that there is less vulnerability for traffickers to exploit. This doesn't mean that it is wrong to migrate, but simply that when people have more choices at home, they are less likely to take risky migration decisions even if they want to leave.

PROSECUTION

LUANA AND MARCELA'S STORY

LUANA: 'A friend of mine told me that a Spanish group was hiring Brazilian girls to work as dancers on the island of Lanzarote. My friend Marcela and I thought it was a good opportunity to earn money. We didn't want to continue working as maids. For a short while we only danced. But later they told us there had been too many expenses. And we would have to make some extra money.'

MARCELA: 'We were trapped by criminals and forced into prostitution in order to pay debts for the trip. We had up to fifteen clients per night. The use of condoms was the client's decision, not ours. The criminals kept our passports and had an armed man in front of the "disco" to make sure we never escaped. But a woman helped us. We went to the police and told everything.'

LUANA AND MARCELA, INTERVIEWED BY THE BRAZILIAN NGO PROJETO TRAMA,
PUBLISHED IN HUMAN TRAFFICKING: AN OVERVIEW, UN (2008)

Given the estimated 2.5 million people subjected to trafficking each year, the numbers of prosecutions and convictions of traffickers in recent years seem shockingly low, as shown in the following two tables.

TRAFFICKING IN PEOPLE

Trafficking in People (TIP) Prosecutions and Convictions by Global Region, 2003–4

REGION/YEAR	PROSECUTIONS	CONVICTIONS
AFRICA		
2003	50	10
2004	134	29
EAST ASIA AND PACIFIC		
2003	1,727	583
2004	438	348
EUROPE AND EURASIA		
2003	2,437	1,561
2004	3,329	1,274
NEAR EAST		
2003	1,004	279
2004	134	59
SOUTH ASIA		
2003	2,599	355
2004	2,705	1,260
WESTERN HEMISPHERE (NORTH AND LATIN AMERICA)		
2003	175	27
2004	145	56
TOTAL	14,877	5,841

'Human Trafficking and Development: The Role of Microfinance', *Transformations*, vol.23, 3 July 2006.

MAKONEN GETU

NUMBER OF CONVICTIONS IN EUROPE

	NUMBER OF CONVICTIONS
Belgium	170
Germany	145
Italy	100
United Kingdom	98
Netherlands	83
Greece	69
Portugal	40
Hungary	39
Austria	27
Latvia	21
Sweden	16
Lithuania	14
Slovakia	14
Czech Republic	12
Estonia	9
Malta	9
Denmark	8
Poland	7
Luxembourg	5
Slovenia	1
Cyprus	–
Finland	–

Bouderwijn de Jonge, *Eurojust and Human Trafficking: the State of Affairs* (Eurojust and University of Amsterdam, 2005).

ACT and unlock freedom for those who are trafficked.

Svetlana was a young Belarusian living in Minsk and looking for a job when she came upon some Turkish men who promised her a well-paying job in Istanbul. Once Svetlana crossed the border, her passport and money were taken and she was locked up. Svetlana and another foreign woman were sent to the apartment of two businessmen and forced into prostitution.

Svetlana had other plans: in an attempt to escape, she jumped out of a window and fell six stories to the street below. According to Turkish court documents, customers did not take Svetlana to the hospital – they called the traffickers instead. These events led to her death. Svetlana's body lay unclaimed in the morgue for two weeks until Turkish authorities learned her identity and sent her body to Belarus.

But Svetlana did not die in vain. Belarusian and Turkish authorities cooperated effectively to arrest and charge those responsible for contributing to a death and for human trafficking.

US DEPARTMENT OF STATE (www.state.gov/g/tip/c16482 htM)

PRESSURE
For our governments ◢

To combat human trafficking on a global scale, it is vital that we pressure our governments to:

◢ Sign and commit to global anti-trafficking legislation and human rights treaties

◢ Pass anti-trafficking legislation that makes the buying and selling of human beings a criminal offence

◢ Enforce the law to prosecute traffickers and those exploiting trafficked people

◢ Fight corruption which encourages and profits from human trafficking

◢ Identify and block trafficking routes through intelligence gathering

◢ Clarify legal definitions of trafficking and coordinate law enforcement responsibilities.

'Human Trafficking and Development: The Role of Microfinance', *Transformations*, vol.23, 3 July 2006.

PROTECTION

To encourage rehabilitation and reintegration into society, it is essential that people who have been trafficked are protected.

They need access to:

▲ **Social services**

▲ **Legal aid**

▲ **Counselling.**

Training police officers and immigration officials is key; this enables them to spot traffickers and assist those who have been trafficked.

But too often, people who have been trafficked are treated as criminals. Imagine enduring the ordeal of trafficking: far away from home, treated like a slave. And then, after the elation of escape, the despair of being treated like a criminal, trapped and confused, again.

People trafficked into the UK are not automatically given a visa to stay. One way of protecting trafficking 'victims' is to allow them visas to stay here in safety – at least until their place of origin is deemed safe. Otherwise, they may be sent straight back to where they came from. This could put them in more danger: their traffickers will very likely hunt them down and harm them, and they may be re-trafficked.

Additionally, some will have come from abusive homes, and sending them away merely sends them home to danger. Others will come from places where they don't earn enough to eat and they will be put back in the same situation which made them vulnerable in the first place.

'Some governments not only fail to recognize the global anti-trafficking legislation and standards, but also punish trafficked people both in destination and origin countries.'

'HUMAN TRAFFICKING AND DEVELOPMENT: THE ROLE OF MICROFINANCE', *TRANSFORMATIONS*, VOL.23, 3 JULY 2006

'I have heard their groans and sighs, and seen their tears, and I would give every drop of blood in my veins to set them free.'

HARRIET TUBMAN (1820–1913), *ESCAPED-SLAVE-TURNED-ABOLITIONIST*

EXAMPLES OF SUPPORT PROJECTS

TRAFFICKING IN RURAL CHINA

Li was trafficked from the market near her village in south-west China where she faced the daily desperation of harsh poverty and the threat to her own survival.

One day, a man told Li he knew her sister, and knew how to take Li to visit her. She was promised transport to an otherwise inaccessible destination. But a life of promise was suddenly turned into a life promising only abuse. Bought as a wife by a wealthy bachelor, Li was forced into a marriage built on a transaction and not on the exchange of committed promises.

She was stolen away from her husband and one year old daughter by this trafficker. A vulnerable woman. A promising profit for a trafficker.

For three years Li was locked in a room when she returned home each day from the fields with the people that guarded her. She was used as a slave for the farm and for sex, taunted by the family of her new owner, beaten, considered nothing. Li promised herself she would escape, she would return to her family.

Uneducated, unable to even speak the local language, that dream of escape seemed beyond her. But one day her chance to escape came true. She ran until she reached a town. She got a job in a factory. She met a woman who spoke her language, a woman who promised to help her, a woman who kept her promises.

Bought as a wife by a wealthy bachelor, Li was forced into a marriage built on a transaction and not on the exchange of committed promises.

Li now lives at home. She is rebuilding her life in a village where there are very few women left. She is once again a real wife, a mother, and she promises herself she will never let her daughter fall into the same trap. As part of a Salvation Army education, awareness and rehabilitation project, Li is now helping to 'stop the traffik' by sharing her story with other villages and communities to make sure they don't fall victim to the same injustice.

INFORMATION TAKEN FROM FACE TO FACE INTERVIEW WITH 'LI'. NAME HAS BEEN CHANGED. WRITTEN IN 2007 BY GRAEME HODGE FOR THE SALVATION ARMY INTERNATIONAL DEVELOPMENT UK. WWW.SALVATIONARMY.ORG.UK/ID

STOP THE TRAFFIK SUPPORTING PROJECTS AROUND THE WORLD

PATH TO FREEDOM

STOP THE TRAFFIK's 'Path to Freedom' initiative is a major new global fund, establishing regionally focused funding initiatives, along human trafficking routes. The projects funded in these initiatives will be interlinked as much as possible and will tackle various dimensions of the human trafficking problem.

In this way the fund will make sure that funding tackles root causes such as poverty and gender discrimination amongst the most vulnerable groups, and targets early intervention and rescues, safe houses, good options for either going home and building a new life or, if that is too dangerous, finding a new place to live and work or study.

Finally, the fund will help frontline professionals follow through on prosecuting traffickers, so that this will not remain a crime with high benefits and low costs. The STOP THE TRAFFIK Path to Freedom initiative is a global fund with a comprehensive approach to making the greatest possible impact.

Path to Freedom will work in regions all over the world. The first of these initiatives is in South Asia, which is one of the world's human trafficking hotspots, with thousands of women, children and men exploited every day. According to the National Human Rights Commission (NHRC), United Nations Development Fund for Women (UNIFEM), International Social Services (ISS), in 2004, at least 400,000 children in India were victims of sex trafficking. While more than 90% of all trafficking in India is internal, there is also a substantial number of women and children who are trafficked from Nepal and Bangladesh into India for sexual exploitation and forced labour.

There is some political will in South Asia to make an impact against human trafficking, with the South Asian Association for Regional Cooperation (SAARC) countries signing a convention in 2000 to fight this crime. In addition to this, South Asian countries have a strong and well-established NGO community that is beginning to act against human trafficking. There is a huge problem, but the foundations are there for making progress in solving it.

NATIONAL ACTION

STOP THE TRAFFIK is a growing global coalition involving clubs, schools, faith groups, businesses and charities around the world.

THE COALITION COVERS OVER 50 COUNTRIES, INCLUDING:

Albania, Australia, Azerbaijan, Bangladesh, Belarus, Belgium, Bulgaria, Burkina Faso, Cambodia, Cameroon, Canada, China, Czech Republic, Eire, Equador, Estonia, Ethiopia, Ghana, Greece, Hong Kong, Hungary, India, Lebanon, Malaysia, Moldova, Nepal, Netherlands, Nigeria, Norway, Pakistan, Philippines, Romania, South Africa, South Korea, Sri Lanka, Thailand, UK, USA and Zimbabwe.

Signing declarations in different ways.

To see a full list of all STOP THE TRAFFIK's partners, visit the website

www.stopthetraffik.org

STOP PRESS... CHOCOLATE CAMPAIGN SUCCESS IN THE NETHERLANDS

In 2007, Fairfood and STOP THE TRAFFIK held a demonstration against the worst forms of child labour in the cocoa industry outside the Dutch parliament. Two parliamentarians joined the demonstration, which marked the end of a competition inviting major producers of chocolate to commit to significant improvement. None of the companies approached were willing to make significant changes and therefore there was no winner of the competition. The protest was widely covered in the national media.

On the same day as the demonstration, Fairfood placed a full-page advert on the back cover of one of the Netherlands' most widely read newspapers. The advert protested against the lack of improvement and transparency by Royal Verkade (owned by United Biscuits) and by Kinder (owned by Ferrero). It was a spoof on the logos of the producers.

The '**naming and shaming**' campaign, which also linked Royal Verkade with the worst forms of child labour in the Ivory Coast, proved to be a major turning point. After the demonstration and advert, both United Biscuits and Ferrero asked for meetings with Fairfood to discuss possible solutions to the worst forms of child labour in their production chain and Royal Verkade made contact with Fairtrade.

'Within a day we had a phone call from Fairtrade,' states Antonie Fountain of STOP THE TRAFFIK Holland, 'saying that Verkade had just called them to talk about the possibility of Fairtrade sourcing for their cocoa.'

In July 2008, Royal Verkade took a **landmark decision** that will result in a **20% increase in Fairtrade – Traffik Free – chocolate worldwide.**

The company announced that it will be using 100% Fairtrade cocoa and sugar in its products from the autumn onwards. This is the first A-list chocolate producer worldwide to make the transition to Fairtrade production on a large scale and Royal Verkade is congratulated for taking this decision.

THIS IS BIG NEWS but it is critical we keep pressure up on this issue. We are making a difference. We will not stop until the trafficking has been STOPPED. **http://www.stopthetraffik.org/getinvolved/act/chocolate**

www.stopthetraffik.org/
chocolatecampaign

STOP THE TRAFFIK'S CALL FOR AN EU HOTLINE

STOP THE TRAFFIK has been campaigning for a European Union (EU) hotline using one number across all the twenty-seven countries of the EU. The idea is that the number routes to the national service of the country you are calling from. Victims of human trafficking sometimes don't even know which country they are in, so even if there is a national hotline they have little chance of knowing it.

When we have one number, everyone has access to it – and when you ring it, it puts you in contact with the service nearest you.

The organization has worked hard to get this concept accepted and the EU Commission is putting it through a feasibility study. In the meantime, the EU Parliament has voted for two million Euros (£1.6 million) to be spent in 2008 strengthening existing hotlines, such as Estonia's Living For Tomorrow (www.lft.ee), in preparation for the EU hotline number.

STOP THE TRAFFIK IN ZIMBABWE

'Socio-economic challenges in Zimbabwe have left a number of people vulnerable to exploitation, as more people are leaving the country in search of better opportunities. Some young girls are moving from the rural area to the urban areas, exposing themselves to domestic servitude and prostitution after false promises of education and living opportunities. People might not be aware that this criminal exploitation is actually happening in their communities, on their very doorsteps.

Oasis Zimbabwe under the Campaign is working in partnership with the International Organization for Migration (IOM), Harare office, to run a national toll-free line for trafficking information and referrals. This hotline will help determine encountered victims of human trafficking and identify local resources available in the community to help victims.

Some organizations are currently working together to establish a referral system on local organizations that will assist victims with counselling, case management, legal advice, and other appropriate services, as well as make referrals to law enforcement agencies in order to help victims. Anti-trafficking working groups have been established from different social services organizations, a move established and facilitated by IOM.

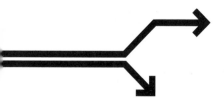

In light of the 2010 World Cup, the working groups are preparing for a nationwide program that will raise awareness on this human exploitation, a lesson learnt from the World Cup in Germany in 2006. Oasis Zimbabwe has been working with IOM since 2006 and has been in partnership with the organization to offer shelter to fourteen- to eighteen-year-old trafficked girls. Oasis Zimbabwe is part of a working group to develop a trafficking manual which will be used by various organizations.

Oasis Zimbabwe would like to see a shelter established for trafficked victims in the near future. Currently most shelters and orphanages in the country are full and some do not have the capacity to take on more people, especially victims of trafficking and migration. We are in the process of looking for funding for such a project. We hope that we can get adequate information through this hotline to help us as part of an active working group to map out what services we need to provide.'

NOMAGUGU MASUKU
STOP THE TRAFFIK ZIMBABWE CAMPAIGN COORDINATOR

BANGLADESH: LANDMARK REPATRIATION OF TRAFFICKED GIRLS

In the past, Bangladeshis who have been rescued from prostitution in India were treated as illegal immigrants and were deported to Bangladesh by the 'push back' method, which meant the girls were taken to the border and pushed across, so they then became the problem of the Bangladeshi government.

A Bangladeshi survivor of trafficking who was rescued from a brothel in Mumbai.

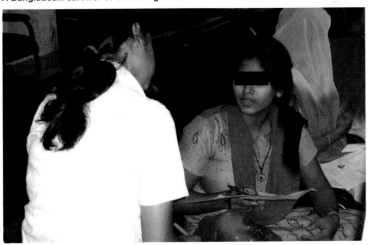

Travel packs were given to each of the girls, which included a new outfit, toiletries and a travel bag.

The girls were often left without help or support and sometimes again became victims of abuse by the border patrol guards.

In April 2008, the South Asia Centre for Missing and Exploited People (SACMEP) took part in a historical event – the first-ever repatriation from Maharashtra state to Bangladesh.

Twenty-two girls and two infants were safely returned to Bangladesh on 21 April 2008.

Excitement was building up in the government homes where the girls were held; some of the girls had wanted to go home for a long time. The girls were in high spirits, and to prepare themselves for the adventure they were putting henna in their hair and on their hands in elaborate patterns.

Travel packs were given to each of the girls, which included a new outfit, toiletries and a travel bag. When asked about the repatriation, the girls answered that they were very happy – especially as they were going on an aeroplane for the first time!

Many of the girls will face stigma from their communities and time needs to be taken to prepare them for this and also to help sensitize the communities.

Many of the girls will not tell their families where they have been and what happened to them in order to protect themselves from rejection and/or ridicule.

SACMEP

Stories like this show that there is hope. Action can be taken, and is being taken, to help people who have been trafficked. Success is possible.

STOP THE TRAFFIK IN INDIA: RECORD-BREAKING MARATHON

A summer event called *Injabulo* (meaning 'joy' in Zulu), including fun and sports, reached out to 700 children/young people across eight communities. During that time they highlighted what trafficking is, largely through sketches performed by staff. For example, one sketch was about child labour (including using children for begging, selling drugs and stealing); another showed women being trafficked for commercial purposes; another depicted the sale of kidneys and other body parts. As a conclusion, it was decided the team should try to break the Marathon Relay Record. And they did – by five seconds!

One-hundred and eighty children (the majority of them were under twelve) and young people, including some from Mumbai and Bangalore, ran the distance in one hour, forty-six minutes and twenty seconds. They created an enormous STOP THE TRAFFIK banner – twenty metres long – as a way of involving the children, young people and their families.

In the evening, the MP Ms Kanimozhi was the chief guest, speaking about how important education is in the current Indian context. Also present was the Additional Director General of Police, Mr Nataraj (a former Commissioner for Human Rights), speaking on anti-trafficking, mentioning that the major cause was poverty and other ignorance – and that it is up to communities to stand up and fight this crime.

COMMUNITY ACTION ◢

As communities, we can help undermine trafficking by starting with three main principles:

1. Awareness raising

2. Advocacy

3. Fundraising and practical support.

Runners before taking part in the second Run for Freedom, held in both Bermuda and London in March 2008.

AWARENESS RAISING

Communities can work together to create increased public awareness of what is, at the moment, a little-known or understood injustice.

STOP THE TRAFFIK has brought together organizations that already work in the field of human trafficking, complementing their efforts through creating a big media 'platform', as well as offering resources to communities for increasing awareness at a local level.

As one voice, communities will effectively touch the public conscience in a stronger, more powerful way than we could individually.

When communities and organizations increase awareness of the dangers of trafficking, this helps to arm people against the charms of traffickers.

Some will still be tempted by traffickers if poverty is still an issue. But information about the brutal reality of trafficking can still empower vulnerable people to avoid risk.

Knowledge helps to give people SAFETY, HOPE and CHOICE.

TOP JOBS ABROAD

Visitors to the Compass Jobs Fair came across a stand for Top Jobs Abroad, a fictional recruitment agency 'offering the very best opportunities'. After being greeted by the friendly representative they were ushered through a door, and straight into a red-light district window – in full view of passers-by. The 'victims' then exited the window onto the official STOP THE TRAFFIK stand and were given further information about the plight of women trafficked into sex slavery through false pretences and were invited to sign the declaration to the UN. STOP THE TRAFFIK's Phil Lane also ran a seminar at the jobs fair programme, raising awareness of this issue.

Watch the Top Jobs Abroad stand at *www.youtube.com/ watch?v=ADTIA asOyhI).*

Top Jobs Abroad stand at the Compass Jobs Fair.

STOP THE TRAFFIK's ongoing Freedom Events help raise awareness about human trafficking. Often they are small, achievable events – but with huge impact.

The first Freedom Day was timed to coincide with the 200th anniversary of the abolition of the trans-Atlantic slave trade. The response was overwhelming, with many local events combining to make a big national impact.

TUNBRIDGE WELLS MARKS FREEDOM DAY

There have been strange goings on in Tunbridge Wells in the UK. One could almost be forgiven for thinking that the spa town was actually living up to its recent accolade of being the fourth happiest town to live in the UK. Not only has the town recently celebrated Fairtrade Town status, but it has, for two years in succession, hosted a community art project, this one based on Fairtrade chocolate. Students from twenty-two of the local schools worked to produce papier maché Easter eggs that were used to dress the trees in the town centre. One shopper commented that: 'This is the sort of thing you find in London or Brighton, but not Tunbridge Wells.' Could it be that the town is being swept away in a newfound taste for the cosmopolitan?

The community art installation, initiated by the Fairtrade Town Group, is based on the ethics of the chocolate industry, seeking not only to highlight the problem of finding Fairtrade Easter eggs in our supermarkets and sweet shops (despite the so-called move of many of the large retailers towards more ethical products on their shelves), but also to turn a spotlight on the huge problem of slavery that still exists in the chocolate industry today.

Fairtrade Campaigner Mandy Flashman-Wells says: 'It is incredible that we are celebrating the 200-year anniversary since the abolition of the slave trade in this country, yet children and adults are still used as slaves on cocoa plantations today.' She adds: 'This project is part of the STOP THE TRAFFIK Campaign – a global voice that is calling for an end to the trade in human traffick across the world.'

The chocolate industry involves vast sums of money, yet the average cocoa farmer earns less each year than the average UK family spends on chocolate.

Papier maché eggs in Tunbridge Wells, UK.

'It is very difficult to buy Fairtrade Easter eggs in Tunbridge Wells and there is little or no Fairtrade chocolate offered as choice at child height. We hope that this huge gap in the market can be conveyed to our shops through this project,' continues Mandy Flashman-Wells.

Whilst it is true that farmers who can sell their cocoa into the Fairtrade market are guaranteed to receive a minimum price, there is insufficient consumer demand for Fairtrade chocolate, so the market for Fairtrade cocoa is limited.

Papier maché eggs hang on a tree in Tunbridge Wells.

Many cocoa farmers have to sell their crop for a price that doesn't even cover the cost of production. For the chocolate industry to be transformed, there needs to be a consumer move towards the more ethically produced Fairtrade chocolate and pressure on the chocolate giants to produce chocolate that is guaranteed Traffik Free. This is the guarantee that cocoa used in the chocolate has not been harvested by trafficked labour.

Mandy Flashman-Wells commented: 'What started out as a simple community art project has turned into something much bigger. When we set out on this project we hadn't realized that we were speaking out for the faceless children enslaved for this country's love affair with chocolate. Our children can enjoy a huge variety of chocolate products which other children have suffered for. The final twist came as we noticed that the last two papier maché Easter eggs to be hung in the trees had faces painted on them. We felt that the unknown children had been given a face by the students in Tunbridge Wells.'

MANDY FLASHMAN-WELLS

ADVOCACY

Advocacy involves giving a voice to the voiceless. It means standing alongside them and addressing those who have the power to make a difference.

Often the form of advocacy with the greatest long-term significance involves not just speaking up on someone's behalf but empowering them to speak up for themselves. STOP THE TRAFFIK and its partner organizations are working not only to speak up for trafficked people but to empower them to do the same.

Through the mouthpiece of the organization, both individuals and communities can call for action from the United Nations, and from individual domestic governments and major corporations, to implement legislation and policies against such injustice.

At the heart of this advocacy is the STOP THE TRAFFIK declaration:

◢ **Prevent the sale of people**

◢ **Prosecute the traffickers**

◢ **Protect the victims.**

We call for increased SAFETY, HOPE and CHOICE for all those affected by human trafficking.

FUNDRAISING AND PRACTICAL SUPPORT

There is a huge range of fundraising activies open to those who want to help combat trafficking. Fundraising events can also help educate by raising public awareness.

You can fundraise for the campaign or for any of the other anti-trafficking organizations featured in the book. Your event needn't be huge or complicated to organize. See pp. 152–3 for some easy and effective ideas.

It's not Wembley Stadium – it's your local community. If there's something you enjoy doing, a gift you have – be it music, dance, sport – maybe you could think of how it could be used in your community to raise some money, and awareness, for trafficked people.

CHARLOTTE WILBERFORCE

Charlotte Wilberforce, the great-great-great-granddaughter of William Wilberforce, continues the fight against slavery. She organized the Run for Freedom in London on 24 March 2007 to raise awareness and funds. In 2008, she organized the Run for Freedom in Bermuda and the UK run on 30 March 2008. **See www.justgiving.com/ londonrunforfreedom.**

Supporters in the Run for Freedom in Bermuda.

START

'We should be taught not to wait for inspiration to start a thing. Action always generates inspiration. Inspiration seldom generates action.'

Frank Tibolt (1897–1989)

1 BECOME AWARE
Understand how trafficking affects your community

◢ If a story in this book has touched you, find out more about the organization who provided that story for this book.

◢ Every year the US State Department publishes on the web a 'Trafficking in Persons Report'. The report lists every country and what they are doing to combat trafficking. Download it and read about the latest on your country.

◢ Download SPOT THE TRAFFIK from www.stopthetraffik.org. Read it and put it in your wallet. If you ever see something that you think indicates a person might have been trafficked, take a look at SPOT THE TRAFFIK and the trafficking indicators, call one of the numbers and report it.

2 TELL OTHERS
Help others understand what trafficking is and how it affects their community

◢ Go to www.stopthetraffik.org and download STOP THE TRAFFIK's logo and web banner. Add them to your e-mail signature, website or blog. The world wide web is a great way of carrying the message that people shouldn't be bought and sold.

3 JOIN THE GLOBAL MOVEMENT
... to STOP THE TRAFFIK or take part in other anti-trafficking campaigns or projects of your choice.

Go to the web and find out what organizations are working to combat trafficking in your country.

Join STOP THE TRAFFIK online at www.stopthetraffik.org to:

◢ **Prevent the sale of people**

◢ **Prosecute the trafficker**

◢ **Protect the victims**

You can receive campaign updates. STOP THE TRAFFIK will keep you updated on fresh STOP THE TRAFFIK ideas and resources to get the message across that people shouldn't be bought and sold.

▉ ACT

Active Community against Trafficking.

STOP THE TRAFFIK is committed to community action. Form a group and take action against trafficking in many different ways

Join our campaigns and use our free downloadable global resources to help you ACT

◢ **Against trafficking in the sex industry**

◢ **Against trafficking in the chocolate industry**

◢ **Against trafficking in the business community**

and launch your own fundraising initiative around the STOP THE TRAFFIK. Raise funds for STOP THE TRAFFIK or one of the other fabulous organizations mentioned in this book.

There is something for everyone to do in their Active Community group (ACT) that will STOP THE TRAFFIK. Go to: www.stopthetraffik.org

David Newton wanted to do something that would get his school thinking about some of the harsh realities of slavery, past and present. He spent seven days non-stop in shackles that weighed about 4 kg.

1 TRAVEL FOR TRAFFIC

Draw the STOP THE TRAFFIK Key on your hand and take a picture of yourself at every tube station, train station, bus stop or landmark in town. Get sponsored for every place you visit in 24 hours.

2 WASH THE TRAFFIC

Hold a car wash and ask for donations. Hold it at a venue with a car park that lots of people drive to, a school event for example.

3 AVOID TRAFFIC FOR A WEEK

Get everyone in your group to walk or cycle instead, or even use rollerblades, scooters and pogo sticks! Any mode of transport is allowed as long as it's not traffic. Save up the money you would have spent and donate it. You'll feel much healthier too.

4 MYSTERY TOUR

People who are trafficked are often taken away from their homes and moved to locations that they don't know. Arrange a mystery tour of your local area for your friends, your class or your youth group. Take them to surprising places and talk about the issue of trafficking. Get them to pay for the privilege!

5 COINS FOR PEOPLE

Get your group to collect small change by giving them a container – something like a clean, empty jar or tube that was used for crisps etc. Get people to cut a hole in the lid and put their small change inside at the end of each day. Set a deadline for when they have to be handed in. Award a small prize to the person who has collected the most as an added incentive to fill the containers!

6 SERVE TEA AND COFFEE

Take responsibility for serving tea and coffee after a school event, church meeting or club evening. Make sure you use Fairtrade products. Ask people for donations for trafficking projects, and use the opportunity to raise awareness too.

Serve them at a coffee morning, fête or after church and raise money for trafficking projects.

8 FIT FOR LIFE

Organize a fun run, aerobic session, swimathon, rocking chairathon or any other similar event to show that all humans deserve freedom and life in all its fullness. Ask for donations or get sponsored for the event.

9 KEYS

Buy a Freedom Key, a symbol of STOP THE TRAFFIK for your keyring. A symbol that you can unlock freedom for those who are trafficked. A reminder of the issue every time you use your keys. Buy bulk, sell on and raise funds.

Thanks to the Salvation Army for these ideas.

Children create a STOP THE TRAFFIK banner, and raise funds through asking people to stick their spare change to the Freedom Key.

TOP TIPS FOR GETTING ORGANIZED

✔ If you are fundraising in a public place, find out about which licence you'll need from your local authority. Don't go door-to-door, collecting sponsors.

✔ Don't put children and young people at risk – make sure they interact only with trusted adults. If children are involved, it will be your responsibility to make sure they are properly supervised and have permission from their parents or guardian. We suggest you may want to get this permission in writing.

✔ When holding a competition, raffle or lottery, please consult the gambling authorities in your area or country. You may need to apply for a licence, and you will need to follow their rules and regulations.

✔ Please ensure any printed publicity for your event includes the line: 'In support of STOP THE TRAFFIK' and include the charity number.

STOP THE TRAFFIK does not authorize fundraisers to act as agents on our behalf and will not assume responsibility for organizing, supervising or hosting fundraising activities. All activities, and participation in them, are at the organizers' and participants' own risk. We do not accept responsibility or liability for any loss or damage to property or for death or personal injury arising out of any fundraising activity relating to STOP THE TRAFFIK, except death or personal injury caused by our negligence.

PLAN WELL IN ADVANCE

◢ Get a group of people together and give them specific responsibilities – like programme, publicity, finance and so on.

◢ It's a good idea to involve someone with prior experience of planning events, as there is a lot to consider.

◢ Meet regularly and make sure that everything is going to plan.

◢ Decide exactly what you want to achieve at the outset and then refer back to this along the way and after the event to ensure that you did it. After the event, consider evaluating what happened and how for future reference.

GET HOLD OF STOP THE TRAFFIK RESOURCES

Contact the office in advance to get hold of relevant merchandise to sell. Go to the website for lots of useful resources: a poster template, litter cards, videos and scripts and PowerPoint presentation, plus lots more!

WORK COLLABORATIVELY

Make enquiries about what else is happening in your community when you are planning your event. Talk to local churches, community groups and schools. Discuss how your plans can compliment one another, or how you can combine forces to put on something bigger.

RECRUIT VOLUNTEERS

Make enquiries about what else is happening in your community. Use resources from the STOP THE TRAFFIK site to inform potential volunteers about the coalition and its aims. There is a PowerPoint presentation and script that you might find useful. Visit local schools, churches and community groups to get people to help you out on the day. You can also build up useful contacts to help you advertise the event itself.

PRACTICAL ORGANIZATIONAL TIPS

SET A BUDGET

Once you have decided what you want to do, work out what all your expenses will be and set a budget. Budgeting is crucial from the start, as planning with limited experience is likely to involve escalating costs. Engaging event organizers needs to be budgeted, too. Think about how you can raise money or get sponsorship. Local businesses, churches or community groups might be willing to help out.

LICENCING

If you are planning on holding an event that includes what is known as 'regulated entertainment', or one in a public area, or if you are planning to sell alcohol, then you may require a licence from your local authority under the Licensing Act.

This applies to all events of any size, irrespective of whether you charge for admission or not. There are some exemptions – check before you start.

If you do not apply for a licence and you should have done so, you are operating outside of the law. Your local authority will be able to advise you on what licence is appropriate but you should allow plenty of time to ensure that you get it completed within the required timescales.

Sometimes getting a licence can take a lot of work and several months to process, depending on your local authority. It may be best to piggy-back an existing event like a fête, so the original organizers take care of the licensing and other health and safety issues.

HEALTH AND SAFETY

Every event organizer has a legal and moral responsibility to ensure the health, safety and welfare of those working at, attending or affected by the event. As an organizer, you will need to look carefully at what you are planning and consider how you will manage health and safety. Your local authority may want to see this documentation before allowing you to use public spaces.

Central to your planning will be a health and safety assessment. This does not need to be over-complicated and the detail will depend on what you are doing. Look at the hazards posed by what you are doing, who could be harmed and how, and what you will do to reduce the risk. If you are organizing a concert, some of the hazards might include noise levels, crowd movement, electrical connections etc.

Check with your local authority to see if they have a simple guide to producing a health and safety assessment. If you are in the UK, see www.hse.gov.uk/pubns/indg163.pdf for a simple guide to producing this assessment. If you are located in a different country, contact your local STOP THE TRAFFIK branch for further details – you will find the contact details on page 158.

You may also need to create an Event Safety Plan. Guides to these might be found in the risk assessment notes. It may cover organzational structures as well as procedures for fire, evacuations, first aid, stewarding, traffic management and so on. If significant numbers of people are involved, the safety angle of events can be problematic, requiring qualified safety personnel at a cost. Fencing, toilets and parking facilities may also need to be considered.

INSURANCE

Any activity should have appropriate insurance. If you are part of a school, church or other organization, you may be covered under existing policies. If not, consider using a specialized broker. Contact your local STOP THE TRAFFIK office on page 158 for further details.

PUBLIC COLLECTIONS

To collect money in the street, or a public place, you will need to obtain a licence from your local authorities. When you apply, they will give you regulations for collecting. As public collections are popular, it is a good idea to get permission well in advance. Think about how you will store, transport and pay in significant sums of money. Have two or more people who are entrusted with taking the money to a safe place.

Donations to STOP THE TRAFFIK general campaign costs can be either given by individual donations via the website donation page, or you can send them to your nearest STOP THE TRAFFIK office. See page 158 for contact details.

Money raised can also be sent to STOP THE TRAFFIK by bank transfer; email the office for details: info@stopthetraffik.org

FOOD AND DRINK

When you sell food at a fundraising event, you must follow food safety laws.

You can obtain guidelines from your local environmental health department. If you are planning to sell alcohol, see the licensing section above. If you do provide food, it is best to limit what's available to packaged snacks and bottled or canned drinks.

◢ Avoid cooking, as the health and safety regulations are tough.

◢ Remember to use Fairtrade foods where possible.

LOTTERIES AND RAFFLES

Lotteries and raffles are games based upon random selection or chance. Players buy (or are given) chances and prizes are distributed according to lots drawn.

You will need direction from the gaming board in your area or country as to the exact rules and regulations for your lotteries, as there are different rules for different lotteries. Contact your local STOP THE TRAFFIK office shown on page 158 for further details.

To keep updated visit:
www.stopthetraffik.org

STOP THE TRAFFIK:
GLOBAL CONTACTS

STOP THE TRAFFIK
International Office
75 Westminster Bridge Road
London
SE1 7HS
UK
Tel: +44 (0)207 921 4258
Email: info@stopthetraffik.org

STOP THE TRAFFIK Australia
c/o The Salvation Army
3rd Floor
130 Little Collins St
Melbourne 3000
Australia
Tel: +61 (0)3 9251 5277
Email: stopthetraffik@gmail.com

STOP THE TRAFFIK Bangladesh
PO Box 8009
Mirpur, Dhaka 1216
Bangladesh
Tel: +88 01713042386 or +88 02
8022730
Email: stopthetraffik.bangladesh@
generalmail.net

STOP THE TRAFFIK Belgium
c/o Oasis Belgium
Gouverneur Verwilghensingel 8 bus 5
B-3500 Hasselt
Belgium
Tel: 0032 (0) 11 22 38 99
Email: Info@oasisbe.org

STOP THE TRAFFIK India
c/o Oasis India
23/2 Kumaraswamy Naidu Road
Fraser Town, Bangalore – 560005
Tel: +91 80 41253505 or
+91 97 41490048
Skype: anita.kanaiya **Email:** Director,
Anti Human Trafficking anita.kanaiya@
oasisindia.org www.oasisindia.org

STOP THE TRAFFIK Netherlands
Postbus 8609
3503 RP Utrecht, The Netherlands
Email: info@stopthetraffik.nl
Website: www.stopthetraffik.nl

STOP THE TRAFFIK USA
EAST COAST
c/o Love 146
P.O. Box 8266
New Haven, CT 06530, USA
Email: info@stopthetraffik.org

STOP THE TRAFFIK USA
WEST COAST
c/o Oasis USA
P.O. Box 2583
Pasadena, CA 91102-2583, USA
Tel: +1 626 447 0400
Email: info@oasisusa.org

STOP THE TRAFFIK CENTRAL USA
The Salvation Army PROMISE Program
[Partnership To Rescue Our Minors
From Sexual Exploitation]
133 South Ashland Avenue
Chicago, Illinois 60607, USA
Tel: +1 312 291 7916 or
+1 312 291 7942
Email: frank_massolini@usc.
salvationarmy.org;
jennifer_mitchell@usc.salvationarmy.org
Web: www.sapromise.org

RECIPE FOR TRAFFICKING

Take one desperate woman,
ripe for exploiting
Remove her opportunities
Soak her in poverty for a lifetime
Throw in a fistful of organized crime

Mix her up
Turn her out
And there you have it:

One woman, pummelled, panicked.
One woman, freshly trafficked.

ACKNOWLEDGMENTS

The authors and publisher would like to thank the following for the use of their images:

Agape International Ministries/www.aim4asia.org: pp. 50, 51 left, middle and top

Amazing Change/www.amazingchange.com: p. 20

Zane Applegate/Oasis Academy, Enfield: p. 128

BMS World Mission/www.bmsworldmission.org: pp. 90, 91

Nick Catling and Carl Bowen: pp. 11 bottom left and right, 82

CHAB DAI/www.chabdai.org: p. 49

Children on the Edge www.ChildrenOnTheEdge.org: pp. 56, 58

Daughters of Cambodia www.daughterscambodia.org: p. 2

Annie Dieselberg/www.nightlightbangkok.com: pp. 25, 44 left, 48, 78

Esther Benjamins Trust/www.ebtrust.org.uk: pp. 26, 55

Gregg School Southampton, UK: p. 127

Graeme Hodge/The Salvation Army 2005: p. 136

Thomas L. Kelly/www.thomaskellyphotos.com: pp. 16, 93 background

Mishelle Kit: pp. 24, 29, 63, 75, 121

Oasis India & SACMEP/www.oasisindia.org: pp. 15, 76, 86, 141, 142

Duncan Parker/The Salvation Army 2005: pp. 12, 23, 31, 43

Pentwortham Gala Day: p. 138

PREDA/www.preda.org: pp. 124, 125

Matthew Robinson: p. 44 right

Hazel Tompson/www.hazeltompson.com: p. 104

True Visions Productions Ltd/www.truevision.com: p. 99

Mandy Flashmann Wells: pp. 145, 146

Charlotte Wilberforce & Rachel Wilberforce Run for Freedom: pp. 143, 147

Lion Hudson

Commissioning editor: Stephanie Heald

Project editor: Miranda Powell

Production manager: Andy Proudfoot

Created and produced by Ivy Contract Limited

With thanks:
STOP THE TRAFFIK would like to thank Layton Thompson for his photography, Jo Wylde for her contribution to the research and writing of this book and the many individuals and organizations who've contributed stories and photographs to make the book what it is.